VIRTUAL
LEARNING

VIRTUAL LEARNING

A Revolutionary Approach to Building a Highly Skilled Workforce

ROGER SCHANK

McGraw-Hill

New York San Francisco Washington, D.C. Auckland Bogotá
Caracas Lisbon London Madrid Mexico City Milan
Montreal New Delhi San Juan Singapore
Sydney Tokyo Toronto

Library of Congress Cataloging-in-Publication Data

Schank, Roger, 1946-
    Virtual learning   :   a revolutionary approach to building a highly
skilled workforce / Roger Schank.
        p.   cm.
    ISBN 0-7863-1148-7
    1. Employees—Training of—Computer-assisted instruction.
2. Computer-assisted instruction.   I. Title.
HF5549.5.T7S3267   1997
658.3'12404—dc21   97-9624
                                                            CIP

McGraw-Hill

A Division of The McGraw·Hill Companies

    2 3 4 5 6 7 8 9 0   DOC/DOC   9 0 2 1 0 9 8 7

ISBN 0-7863-1148-7

The acquiring editor for this book was Jeffrey Krames, the editing supervisor was Donna
Namorato, and the production supervisor was Suzanne Rapcavage. It was set in
Palatino Roman by Jana Fisher through the services of Barry E. Brown (Broker—Editing,
Design and Production).

Printed and bound by R. R. Donnelley & Sons Company.

McGraw-Hill books are available at special quantity discounts to use as premiums and
sales promotions, or for use in corporate training programs. For more information,
please write to the Director of Special Sales, McGraw-Hill, 11 West 19th Street, New
York, NY 10011. Or contact your local bookstore.

C O N T E N T S

Chapter 13

How People Will Learn In The Future   163

INTRODUCTION

INTRODUCTION

It would be nice if this book created a learning revolution in organizations throughout the world. That's a pipedream, of course, because revolutions aren't created by books. Such books do, however, provoke revolutionary thoughts. Karl Marx, Thomas Paine, and other provocateurs have used the printed word to convey the need for radical change and to catalyze discussion, debate, and experimentation. I suppose I'm trying to do the same.

If I've learned anything in my 15 years working with all types of companies, both U.S. and international, it's that companies' learning systems are bankrupt. The way managers attempt to help their people acquire knowledge and skills has absolutely nothing to do with the way people actually learn. Trainers rely on lectures and tests, memorization and manuals. They train people just like the schools teach students: Both rely on "telling," and no one remembers much that's taught and what's told doesn't translate into usable skills. As this book will make clear, we learn by doing, failing, and practicing. Because most organizations can't afford massive on-the-job failure and most people don't learn when they fail in public, we need to create a safe place to fail and learn—the virtual reality of computer simulations and role playing scenarios serve that purpose.

This stuff scares people. Some success-minded executives don't like the F word (*failure*). Some tradition-minded training managers don't like the prospect of junking their classrooms and manuals. Add such strange notions as "learning should be fun" into the mix and you're bound to get people calling for your head.

Because I'm calling for a revolution, it seems fair to begin by explaining how I became a revolutionary.

WHY COMPUTERS DON'T GET BORED

Like a lot of kids, I despised school. From kindergarten through college, I was asked to commit mountains of trivia to memory and given multiple choice tests to determine whether I had "learned" this trivia. I saw no point to memorizing geometric theorems, the capitals of the world or the names of geologic formations. It was much more fun playing football, going out with girls and tinkering with computers. Knowing I wasn't going to make a living from the first two endeavors, I focused on computers and in graduate school, linguistics. At Stanford University I became a professor of computer science and linguistics, researching how computers might understand language. I moved on to Yale and pursued this rather esoteric discipline, developing a reputation for enabling computers to understand newspaper stories. As I gained some expertise in this area, I made two interesting discoveries, one related to computers and one related to my children:

- **Computers didn't get bored**. I remember that there was a newspaper story in the late '70s about an earthquake in Iran that the computer read repeatedly (because sponsors would ask us to demonstrate it). Why didn't it respond and tell us that it was bored with this story or at least note that there sure were a lot of earthquakes in Iran? Because it didn't remember what it read. It struck me that people become smarter and more sophisticated over time because they read and experience different things and remember them. Building computer programs that became smarter over time seemed a worthwhile endeavor. To do this I studied how people become smart: I studied learning—not school learning, but real life learning. I studied how people learn about restaurants, about terrorism, about car accidents. As I worked on this, I amassed a great deal of experience about how computers and people learn and are able to use what they remember in real life.
- **The gap between what I learned about learning and how and what children are taught in school was enormous**. As I watched my children go through school, I was amazed at the way in which the schools taught them. They were just as bored as I was, but now

I could analyze the problem. They were being called upon to memorize many useless facts under stressful conditions, information they promptly forgot the following year when they had to memorize a new set of useless facts. They were being told what to learn independent of their desire to know it. Real learning takes place by doing, but they weren't doing anything! They needed to be placed in situations where they could make mistakes and practice skills until the students got them right, but they never got to make real mistakes, only artificial mistakes like not knowing the answer to a question that they weren't interested in knowing in the first place.

It dawned on me that I might be able to do something more useful with my expertise than building smart computer programs. I had a team at Yale that understood both computer science and how humans learn and thus would be fully capable of creating educational software to help students learn the right way. We could design programs that would be as fun as any computer game, that would start with goals that children actually had, that would accommodate personality differences (which affect how people learn) and would allow them to make mistakes without feeling humiliated (and in this way search for explanations about why they failed and start them thinking).

It was a terrific idea. Unfortunately, no one in the world of education thought so. The politics and problems associated with revolutionizing the educational system deserve their own book. Still, the evolution of the ideas in this book started with software for the schools. While I was seeking funding for kids software I met some executives from Andersen Consulting. They weren't particularly concerned with the schools, but they were vitally concerned about finding a better way to train their people in critical work skills. Not only a better way, but a faster and cheaper way.

So Andersen brought our team to Northwestern University in 1989. Andersen enjoyed a long-standing relationship with the school (Arthur Andersen himself went to Northwestern and was the chairman of the Board of Trustees) and both recognized the importance of the learning sciences. With the additional backing of the Department of Defense and other federal agencies, Andersen helped fund the Institute for the Learning Sciences (ILS) at Northwestern. ILS today is composed of 200 people, including a mixture of computer scientists, education and psychology professors, and students. Though part of our mandate at ILS is to offer an undergraduate and graduate program, we spend a great deal of time attempting to invent new learning technologies. We also have a for-profit company, Learning Sciences Corporation (LSC), that adapts the technologies we've built at ILS for use by corporate clients. Together we've created both software and role-playing scenarios for a wide variety of organizations. Although other organizations create multimedia programs for corporations, most do little more than transfer classroom formats and manuals to the computer screen. Our goal at both ILS and LSC is quite different. We want to change the way learning works in organizations. Expressed another way, we want to change the way workers learn.

WHAT I'VE LEARNED ABOUT LEARNING

Doing what I've been doing for 15 years, I bring a unique perspective to organizations and their training needs. My background as an academic, learning theorist, and computer scientist is different from most people in the business world. What MBAs and veteran business executives take for granted, I've seen with fresh eyes. I've noticed three facts that compelled me to write this book:

- **People hate training.** With a passion. Viewed as a necessary evil by management and with disdain by employees who go through the process, training is a joke in many companies. It's also a costly joke, given the money and time invested in it. It struck me that there has to be a better way to train people than replicating the educational model that schools rely on and that most intelligent observers and participants agree is broken.

- **People like multimedia technologies.** People like the fact that multimedia is high tech, glitzy and fun to use. Multimedia training is beginning to catch on all over the world—the State of Victoria in Australia actually has a "multimedia minister." The bad news is that much of the multimedia training out there is no better than the old low-tech training; it just looks better. Still, there's great receptivity to computer-based training programs.

- **It's easier to sell to the pocketbook than to the mind.** When I first began pitching my ideas to business, they must have thought I was talking Martian. At the beginning, I'd visit companies and say something to the effect of, "Let me look around and see whether I can find an interesting problem I'd like to work on." As an academic, I was trained to search for interesting problems. Organizations, of course, were only interested in practical solutions. Though managers were intrigued when I explained how it is impossible to learn unless you expect something to occur and it fails to occur (*expectation failure*) and how the stories their employees tell in bars are great learning tools, the managers didn't give me something interesting to work on either. It was only when my team focused on the cost and time savings that our business took off. Organizations immediately understood the benefits of putting their training on "portable" computer disks and keeping their experts out of the classroom and in the field.

All this demonstrated that there was a market for a new, computer-based approach to training, and I was gratified to see organizations incorporating our learning theory and software into their training. At the same time, I was a bit frustrated when the cost-savings and computer bells and whistles took precedence over the ideas. After the fact—after our systems are installed and running—organizations recognize that the real benefit is increased effectiveness. Before that, though, there aren't many true believers. Time after time, I've heard human resources (HR) people say, "It's amazing to watch people acquire skills that used to be so hard to teach. This stuff actually works!"

I understand the initial skepticism. Companies bring in consultants without being fully convinced that their training will become more effective; it's enough that managers know a plan will help them reduce costs. Teaching-by-telling propagandists have brainwashed most of us. It's difficult to make the jump to a learning-by-doing mindset.

Although a book might not help you make that jump, it will at least make you aware that there is another option. I'm not going to dwell on how Learning Sciences Corporation will save your organization oodles of time and money; that's sales presentation stuff. Instead, I want to show you how people really learn and why organizations that embrace this learning approach will have more highly skilled employees than their competitors enjoy.

Of course, showing is the hard part, because this is a book rather than a computer screen.

I'LL TELL YOU SOME STORIES INSTEAD

In an ideal world, a piece of software would accompany this book that would enable you to experience some computer simulations first-hand. You would be thrown into scenarios just as trainees are; you'd be asked to make decisions and solve problems related to skills like coaching, customer service, and selling; and you would invariably make mistakes. When you messed up, you would have alternatives about what to do next. You could get a coach to come on the screen and give you advice; you'd be able to do some research; you could ask specific questions; you could hear an expert tell a story related to your failure; or you could start over and try again. Navigating your way through a simulated work environment, you could easily imagine how the simulation feels like the real thing to training participants; how they could get angry, upset, confused, challenged, entertained and rewarded as they move through the "plot."

Unfortunately, you can't experience this directly. Part of the problem is cost. The development cost for creating a CD-ROM simulation is significant—at least, it's more than most software that accompanies books, making the purchase price prohibitively expensive for some of you. The other problem is equipment. You need the right hardware to run computer simulations. Although some companies may have this equipment, others do not and the individual reader's home computer system probably isn't sufficiently powerful.

As a result, I'm going to have to tell you about things. At its worst, telling is boring, pedantic, forgettable—choose your own negative adjective. At its best, it's entertaining. Think about your favorite high school or college teacher. The odds are he or she was someone who could tell a great story, who made you laugh, who expressed controversial opinions. Throughout this book, I use storytelling, humor, and controversy to make the messages as memorable as possible. Still, sometimes I'll slip into a telling mode. It's inevitable. Once my ex-wife, who's a therapist, told me about a patient who was exhibiting neurotic behavior that seemed eminently curable. After listening to my ex-wife describe all the nutty things her patient was doing, I said, "Why don't you just tell him to stop this nonsense?" It was a reflex response. Unconsciously, perhaps, I thought she could just rationally point out the odd aspects of her patient's behavior and he would understand and be cured. In reality, you can no more talk a neurotic out of neuroses than you can talk an unknowledgeable worker out of ignorance.

Therefore, forgive me in advance for telling you too much and showing you too little. I hope the stories and other entertaining and provocative aspects of this book more than compensate for the limitations of the medium.

WHAT I REALLY THINK ABOUT COMPUTERS

Because so much of what I have to say about learning relates to computers, let's talk a bit about them.

First, even if there were no such thing as a computer, it wouldn't change my views on how people learn. In fact, the existence of computers notwithstanding, a great way to learn is by looking over someone else's shoulder. You can't beat an apprenticeship for teaching you the ropes. Computer simulations are necessary because apprenticeships are impractical and learning on the job can be dangerous from financial and physical perspectives. To learn, you need an environment in which to learn. Virtual learning takes place in a virtual environment.

Second, the learning approach I put forth in this book can still be used even if your organization can't afford to create computer software and buy the hardware. Though I prefer computer simulations to role-playing scenarios for reasons I'll discuss, the latter can still be a highly effective training tool.

Third, *computer-based training* is a meaningless term. Computer-based or multimedia-based training is all the rage, but most of what's on the market has no more to do with learning than penmanship has to do with good creative writing. Some of the programs I've seen feature great graphics, display nifty interfaces, and are as computer-friendly as a cyberdog. But you couldn't learn to train your dog from them. They're electronic training manuals. Instead of reading about policies and procedures in a notebook, you read about them on a computer screen. Our team was once talking to a company leader about designing the training program, but the manager decided to go with another firm. This decision surprised us, not only because companies usually choose us over competitors but because this prospect told us that our computer simulations seemed far more sophisticated and effective than the other firm's. Why then, we asked, did he give our competitor his business? He replied, "Well, its computer software looked a lot like our old training. We didn't want to do anything too different that would rock the boat."

That's a good way of introducing the computer-based training and virtual learning theory behind this book: They rock the boat.

What often rocks traditionalists the most is the virtual aspect of our approach. They just can't accept that training can work without the tools of the training trade—the classroom and manual. *Virtual learning*, therefore, strikes them as nonsense. It may be a slightly silly phrase, but it's not nonsense. The title of this book is a bit of a misnomer—you either learn something or you don't, and virtual learning connotes almost-but-not-quite learning. Still, virtual learning also suggests that learning can take place in cyberspace, in an environment that's one step removed from a real one. It also conveys the learning potential of role-playing goal-based scenarios, live reproductions of real work situations. The point is, employees learn work skills by simulating reality. Perhaps more to the point, employees can learn them faster, cheaper, and more effectively in simulations than in the classroom.

WHO IS THIS BOOK FOR?

Training isn't just for trainers anymore. As organizations have come to appreciate the importance of learning and knowledge as competitive tools, their training approaches have taken on greater importance. Helping employees acquire critical skills quickly and effectively has become a key organizational objective, not just a training goal.

For those reasons I expect and hope that this book will appeal to a cross-section of readers. Certainly trainers and human resource managers will find the material here directly applicable to what they do every day. It offers an alternative approach that can help them train people more effectively and capitalize on multimedia-based tools. At the same time, the book should strike a chord with managers outside of the human resource department. Functional department heads constantly complain about how long it takes to get their people up to speed or how often they screw up. CEOs and other executives are well aware that highly skilled companies are highly successful companies; that if the executives find a way to deploy essential skills to employees better than their competitors do, they will have a huge advantage.

For these reasons, I've written this book for the people who train and for the people who recognize the strategic implications of a superior training method.

1

THE DAMAGE UNDONE:

Remedying the Problems
Caused by Bad Training

It's amazing how many people don't know how to do their jobs properly. Think about your own company and how many times people screw up daily. Television's Homer Simpson may be a caricature, but many employees reflect his cartoonish bewilderment about how to do the job right. This lack of knowledge isn't confined to people on the line or in junior positions. Organizations are filled with employees who haven't been doing their jobs long enough to have really mastered their intricacies. Even the CEO is often barely aware of what is going on in the organization. He or she may not even know what employees are supposed to do. Such a CEO certainly wouldn't know how to do most of the jobs he or she manages.

The result of all this: A day doesn't go by without customers being sent the wrong products, service reps providing callers with inaccurate information, deadlines being missed or overlooked, and someone pushing the wrong key on a computer terminal and mucking up a critical system. And these are just the visible problems. Many screw-ups go undetected at first because it's hard to keep track of everyone in a large organization (plus, if people are expert at nothing else, they're expert at covering up their mistakes).

1

Incompetence is damaging our productivity and profitability. Think about your recent interactions with representatives of airlines, rental car companies, large retail chains, restaurants, hotels, and repair services (from cars to consumer electronics). Were you appalled at the service you received? Was it abysmally slow? Did the person you interacted with know what he or she was talking about? Did you receive the information you required when you required it? Did you get promised one thing and receive another? Did it work when you finally got it home?

Let me share with you a few of my own experiences, both personal and professional:

- I was flying to Barcelona by way of Madrid using a ticket sent to me by the Spanish government that had been bought in pesetas. I decided to reroute the trip through Paris. I made my request at the airline ticket counter and the airline reps went nuts. They became increasingly frustrated and frantic as they attempted to figure out the new fare, factoring in exchange rates, supersaver fares, special discounts, and penalties. Finally the airline representative handed me a ticket and said, "That will be $100." $100 even? That seemed unlikely and I was about to ask whether that was correct, when it dawned on me that she had made the fare up! The world of airline travel has become amazingly complex, and no one had given this person the knowledge and tools necessary to deal with this complexity.

- Perhaps you've had an experience like the mysterious case of the missing fax. I was waiting in a hotel for a fax that my assistant assured me she had sent. When I called down to the hotel desk, however, the person there told me it had not arrived. I then engaged in one of those absurdist dialogs better suited to a Pinter play than to a customer interaction:

  Me: When the fax arrives, please deliver it to my room.
  Clerk: We can't deliver it if you're not there.

Me: I'll be there. But even if I weren't, you could just put it under the door.
Clerk: But the maid might pick it up and throw it away.
Me: You've got to be kidding.

He wasn't. Three hours later the fax was still missing. So I called the manager and instructed him to find the fax. And after a thorough search, he did find it. Apparently it had been faxed to the number for hotel business rather than the one for hotel guests, and it had been sitting for hours in a corner of the reservations desk. Did no one see this fax for a guest and think to deliver it? Perhaps people at the desk had not been instructed in what to do with an undelivered fax, though one shudders to think what else they had failed to learn.

- One company I know trains its restaurant managers by having them work at each of nine "stations" and giving them multiple-choice tests on various policies and rules such as: How often should the washrooms be cleaned: (A) Every 20 minutes. (B) Every 25 minutes. (C) Every 30 minutes. It's difficult to train managers; it's much easier to get them to answer multiple choice questions. The idea that there is a "correct" answer to this question is a little frightening in itself. The idea that there are answers and that memorizing them helps productivity is rather bizarre when one considers the real-life situations these managers face. When the restaurant is hopping, one of the cooks has called in sick, and people in line are starting to grumble about the long wait, that manager needs to be able to prioritize the 15 things that are demanding his attention, not remember that he has 12 minutes until he has to have the washroom cleaned. When the cook calls in sick, managers in this restaurant respond by taking the place of the cook, because the training they received included how to be a cook. Unfortunately, this leaves the restaurant without a manager during crisis time. The restaurant chain's training, however, doesn't take this problem into account.

PROBLEM AREAS: WHERE DUMB THINGS HAPPEN

When people don't know how to do their jobs effectively, organizations feel the impact in multiple, negative ways. High levels of incompetence affect everything from morale to productivity to teamwork. Perhaps the best way to gauge the impact, though, is by focusing on three critical areas.

Let's start with sales. In the old days, salespeople had a simpler, easier job. Then, they usually sold products or services with distinct benefits to established customers, and the competition for those customers was far less fierce than it is today. You didn't have to be a genius to be a good salesperson. Now the environment is much more complex. Given commodity products and services, salespeople have to work extremely hard to get prospects interested and to keep customers buying from them rather than from other sources. Understanding and dealing with customers' attitudes is difficult; the psychology of selling a particular product to a particular customer base is not easily mastered. Most organizations haven't equipped their salespeople to address the complexities of their jobs. More than laziness, lack of talent, or indifference, it is absence of knowledge in highly complex situations that inhibits sales effectiveness.

The second area involves management of employees. What do you do when a subordinate isn't working hard? In the old days, you'd say, "Hey, work harder or you're out of here." Now motivating and disciplining are much more complicated. You have to know the organization's official and unofficial rules for counseling and coaching, for reprimanding and firing. You need motivational skills and conflict management expertise; you require the ability to manage teams and build consensus.

Not many managers possess these abilities. They may have been taught them, given rules to memorize, or listened to lots of lectures on the proper way to do these things, but they haven't learned what they need to know. Not to get ahead of myself, but I should note that "management by buzzword" seems to be the rule rather than the exception in this area. Books get hot, their concepts are turned into training courses, and managers try to memorize the principles and precepts of those courses. There's nothing wrong with "management by walking around," "the one-minute manager" or "change agentry." The problem is that most managers still spend most of their time sitting on their duffs, take forever to make decisions, and are spooked by change. *Knowing* the seven habits of highly effective people and *applying* those habits well throughout your organization are two entirely different things.

Finally, there's the decline and fall of customer service. Toll-free 800 service operators are dealing with random problems of such magnitude and variety that if the operators can't punch in a code and get an answer from their computer, they're lost. It's not just that they can't provide the information a customer needs. It's that no one has taught them how to be empathetic; how to think about a complaint; how to react to a random set of personalities and issues; how to stay cool and effective when a situation becomes emotional; or how to think on their feet and come up with a creative, original solution. When customers depart from the script (which customers do more often than not), service representatives are lost. They have been trained to be robots, and robots aren't flexible or creative.

A little knowledge, imparted properly, could go a long way to solving the problems in these three areas.

Unfortunately, it's not being imparted properly.

WHY DO WE SPEND ALL THAT MONEY ON TRAINING?

Theoretically at least, training should solve the problems just discussed. It's perfectly reasonable to expect an organization's often-sizable investment in training to pay off in competence. Top management has a lot riding on this being the case. Slowly but surely managers are recognizing training's critical role, not just as a cost-of-doing-business necessity, but as a way to gain a competitive advantage. All of this makes it even more frustrating when training fails to meet its objectives.

But wait, the defender of the training faith might be saying, We use state-of-the-art, multimedia-based training. We send our people to executive development programs at the top business schools. We have our own in-house teaching university. We have tests that measure what people in our training programs learn, and they generally test quite well.

To these defenders I would respond: *Training won't teach your people their jobs as well as my grandfather learned his when he apprenticed as a watchmaker.*

Apprenticeships Versus Schooling

During his apprenticeship grandfather learned by looking over the master's shoulder and trying his hand at his chosen trade. I am sure he screwed up a few watches while he learned, but eventually he learned the job through trial and error. There's no substitute for learning-by-doing.

The medieval concept of apprenticeships survived as a teaching tool until relatively recently, when the giganticism of the modern workplace made true and de facto apprenticeships impractical. The master salesperson can't have hundreds of apprentice salespeople dogging his footsteps; the master MIS person can't have hordes of neophyte techies crowded around her computer, for several reasons:

- It's logistically difficult to have the right master available for the right apprentice. In large organizations, people are spread out over many offices in locations around the country or the world. Masters are also traveling more than ever before.
- In addition, the true expert's time is extraordinarily valuable; the time it would take to tutor an apprentice is time taken away from the organization's immediate needs. Some might argue that mentoring is the modern form of apprenticeship, but I'd disagree. In many cases, mentors confine their advice to career and political issues.
- In other instances, a mentor provides only general guidance, because they are unable or unwilling to offer the opportunity for the mentor to follow the prodigies around, observe them in action, and practice their skills under the mentor's watchful eye.

Thus, training. Everything that's wrong with training can be stated in four words: *It's just like school*.

The educational model in schools does not work. That fact, however, hasn't deterred business from adopting this model. The model is based on the belief that people learn through listening. Memorize the teacher's words; memorize the training book's policies and procedures.

It's at this point in my public talks that audience members rise up in protest. Some claim that they learned a great deal in school. To them I ask: If I were to pull out a biology test from high school, how many questions do you think you could answer correctly? Some 99 percent of all my audiences agree that they could not pass a high school biology test if they were given one right then. And the other 1 percent are wrong; I typically carry a test with me to prove the point.

School isn't really about learning; it's about short-term memorization of meaningless information that never comes up later in life. The school model was never intended to help people acquire practical skills. It is intended to satisfy observers that knowledge is being acquired (for short periods of time).

Our major universities—the ones that parents dream about their children attending—were originally created to produce theologians. The rich people who went to Yale and Harvard often went into the family business rather than becoming theologians, but their training in the classics was not intended to provide them with business skills. The classics were taught to create liberally educated gentlemen who presumably would learn about real life somewhere else. The idea has persisted that school should provide a "general education." I was on the faculty at Yale for 15 years. When I was chairman of the computer science department I was asked (along with the heads of other departments) to speak to incoming freshmen about the advantages of majoring in my discipline. Other department heads talked grandly about how they would broaden students' worldview and create well-rounded young men and women. Instead I said, "Major in computer science and you'll get a job." You would have thought that I had committed some terrible sin (which perhaps I had). "We're not a technical school," the university leaders criticized. "We offer a classic liberal arts education." Such thinking is why there are so many unemployed English and philosophy majors. This educational model from 1850 is not one well-suited to training people to obtain key skills.

Why the Educational Model Pervades Companies

There are other objections to my argument, of course. People tell me that philosophy or some other course taught them "how to think." Didn't they know how to think before they took philosophy? A good deal of cognitive dissonance is at work here. Because people labored so diligently at school for so many years, they convince themselves that there must have been a lot of learning going on. Although these people might admit there are problems with schools, they attribute those problems to "sex, drugs, and rock and roll." The basic model is sound, they believe. As a result, they replicate it in work situations.

They're able to replicate it because the people who did well in school tend to be the heads of companies or occupy other powerful positions. What worked for them should work for others, they reason. Only it doesn't (and it "worked" for most of them because they were grinds or had good memories; it's debatable whether a Harvard grad has more work skills than a high school dropout). We end up with Motorola University, Intel University, and Quaker University—with instructors trying to tell people how to work using the same lecture-and-memorize techniques.

When I began my relationship with Andersen Consulting, the firm's trainers relied on green-covered manuals to teach new hires about the firm's approach to accounting and management. The green books delivered information in dry, dull-as-toast prose (remarkably like school textbooks). Everyone was bored by and hated these books;. my first recommendation to Andersen was to destroy them.

My next recommendation was to start learning by doing. How Andersen did so I'll save for later. For now, let's consider why organizations like Andersen are willing to depart from traditional training methods.

WHEN ALL ELSE FAILS . . .

When managers of an organization come to us and say "help!" they are usually facing significant problems that can't be solved through training that tells. For instance, we delivered a course for the Veterans Administration (VA) hospitals focused on chief-of-staff training. In the old days, chiefs of staff "grew up" in hospitals, working their way up the administrative ranks and learning what the directors had to learn. Today, these people jump from hospital to hospital, never staying long enough to acquire the skills necessary to manage institutions that are changing and growing. Combined with the government's insistence that the VA become profitable, these hospitals desperately need leaders who have their jobs down cold.

Similarly, managers of a British water utility company came to ILS hoping that we could teach their people to communicate clearly with customers and treat them like human beings. Like many utilities throughout the world, the utility was struggling to differentiate itself from a growing number of competitors. It occurred to these managers that their only real point of competitive difference was service, and that the company's service stank.

Andersen Consulting, the $4-billion business consulting firm, believes that training its people is the cornerstone of the business. It was clear that all the manuals and other training tools couldn't convey the intricacies of a consultant's life. Andersen might hire the most brilliant consultants in the world, but how can they learn to sell that brilliance to prospective customers? With an ambitious growth strategy in place, Andersen can't afford mediocrity and incompetence in any critical area.

Andersen, the British water utility, and the VA, like many organizations today, are facing crises. If they don't find a better way to teach people how to do their jobs, the organizations are headed for serious trouble. Many times, it takes a major problem—and the inability of traditional training methods to solve that problem—to catalyze a new way of thinking. It shouldn't be so difficult. Unfortunately, the myths and misconceptions about training and education keep many organizations clinging to the status quo.

THE THREE BIG TRAINING FEARS

It's scary how top executives raise objections and concerns about new training approaches. In these ways executives prevent organizations from addressing critical mass problems. Managers in most organizations recognize that their current training isn't working, but they resist the notion that their training model is fatally flawed. As a result, they look to variations on the training-as-telling theme. They'll use computer-based learning methods to train their people; they'll implement intensive workshops that compress learning; they'll train employees as part of teams; they'll bring in various gurus who are experts at motivation, learning, and leadership. But when you strip away all the bells and whistles, the trainers are still trying to tell people what they need to know, and that strategy is doomed.

Yet organizations are afraid to try new approaches. See whether the following three fears are familiar:

- **It will take too long and cost too much**. After presenting LSC's training concept to managers, many of them will ask the same question: "Can't we do it faster?" The old educational model provides the false comfort of definable time and cost expenditures: It will take one week and $10,000 to teach 100 employees using Manual X. A learning-by-doing approach isn't so easy to define. Many jobs are complex; they take a while to learn. "Do we really have to do all that?" the managers ask. People get crazed about the time and money they have to spend "on training of all things," which brings up the next point.
- **It's not effective**. Training departments are second-class citizens in many companies. Rightly or wrongly, CEOs view training departments as the home of old schoolteachers and other corporate misfits—the businesspeople don't trust them. And it's true that

training's general ineffectiveness has biased
management against the discipline. For CEOs focused
on short-term earnings, long-term knowledge gains
frequently aren't a high priority.

- **It can't be measured**. In other words, managers want
training to be like school, with a series of standardized
tests that measure progress and success. Organizations
that use traditional training can at least test employees
and see how much knowledge they retained from a
course—not that it means anything, because facts
memorized are facts quickly forgotten. Real learning is
difficult to measure through standardized tests. How do
you measure whether a service representative is more
empathetic or whether a manager has developed the
ability to prioritize? The only way to do so is by
observation and long-term gains in productivity and
profitability.

THE GOOD NEWS

As bad as training has been and as mistake-prone as the U.S.
workforce is, the opportunity is there for organizations to reverse this situation. Most organizations harbor experts in various areas who possess priceless knowledge. The key is to
transfer that knowledge to employees in the right way at the
right time.

This transfer can be facilitated if companies accept some basic premises of learning.

First and Foremost: When Learning Isn't Fun, It's Not Learning

The movies, for all their faults, usually get this idea right. In the
film *The Dead Poets Society*, Robin Williams plays a teacher who
jumps on top of desks, makes the class laugh, tells great stories,
and gets the class involved in what he's teaching them. The educational establishment at the school hates the way Williams
teaches, based on the premise that if it's fun, it's bad. Listening

to endless lectures and memorizing countless facts and figures aren't fun activities.

What's fun is *doing*. As ensuing chapters demonstrate, computer simulations or noncomputerized role-playing offers people the chance to participate, to make mistakes, to take chances, to challenge themselves, and to learn.

To make this revolutionary notion a reality, however, managers have to ask themselves some tough questions about training. Specifically:

- What do you teach?
- Why do you teach it?
- How do you teach it?
- Are you sure that's what you want to teach?

For now, let's talk about the first question. Most of us know the low-level skills and tasks that trainers need to teach our people. What stump us are the more complex skills and tasks. And whether managers like it or not, the modern workplace is filled with complex job responsibilities. People need to know how to manage a team in which five people are at each other's throats. They need to develop improvisational skills to satisfy a customer when the answer to a question isn't obvious. On top of that, organizations have grown so large that employees are dealing with a mind-boggling number of products and services and a complex system of processes and policies. If that isn't enough, downsizing frequently increases the individual workload and skill demands. An employee may need to be trained to do the work and use the skills that formerly were divided among two or more employees.

The person who's best-equipped to help these people may not be available to do so. The expert for any given product or situation may be stationed in London or may not even be in the company any more; you can't just run down the hall and ask him a question or learn by looking over his shoulder. The need for capturing and delivering this knowledge effectively is great.

But let's return to the "what" question. What managers want people to learn isn't limited to subject matter or clearly definable skills. Attributes and values are also crucial. It's fine to teach a salesperson what she needs to know about the products she's selling, but trainers also need to teach her how to communicate with customers. That doesn't mean instructors give her a lecture or workbook listing the 10 rules of communication; rather, trainers must create simulated situations where she can practice communicating. That salesperson also needs to practice active listening skills, time management techniques, and ways to interpret body language. None of these are as easy as just teaching her about her product, but they're absolutely necessary.

The good news is that most of these skills can be mastered with practice. Even though some learning may seem daunting, it can be accomplished if the right learning environment is created. A good analogy has to do with teaching people to program a VCR. Perhaps someone you know is a technophobe—you might as well ask him to build a rocket as to program the VCR. No matter what advice you give him or how he studies the instruction manual, the task just seems too complex. But when you create an environment that allows this person to practice and fail at programming, with help when needed and in a situation where he really wants to master the skill (perhaps his all-time favorite movie is on), eventually he'll master it.

The only learning that a person can't master is when a skill is completely new and no experience or expertise exists to guide the learning. Organizations sometimes tell us they're launching a new system of some sort, and they want us to build a training program to go along with the system. That's very difficult to do. Without the knowledge of mistakes made and solved, without real expertise to guide us, we have to design training in the dark. Effective training requires real experience for use as a guide. We learn best from reality.

Most of the time, however, the issue is raising the level of expertise on existing systems. This issue is exacerbated by the increased movement of people from one organization to the next—by the time someone learns a job well, he or she is off to the next job. It would be ideal if organizations could afford to let these people learn on the job; if novices had the luxury of making mistakes like my apprentice watchmaker grandfather did. But in our highly competitive business climate, mistakes are too costly. Still, organizations persist in throwing people into situations they haven't been trained to handle and hoping against hope that they can "get the hang of it." This false hope is the reason so many star athletes fail as managers—their experience has only prepared them to play, not to manage. It's also why I get so nervous whenever we elect a United States president who wasn't previously vice president—being governor of a state isn't adequate training. It takes a good year or two before any new president learns the ropes—he too is learning by failing—but in the president's case, failing can be quite costly (not to mention dangerous).

There's a better way to prepare people to do a competent job, and as the following chapters demonstrate, it's one that every organization can use to deal with the major problems they face.

2 CHAPTER

SIMULATING WORK:

Creating Ideal Learning Environments

Learning-by-doing is easier said than done. John Dewey recognized this way back in 1916 when he noted that schools insist on telling students what they need to learn despite research clearly demonstrating that learning by telling doesn't work and learning-by-doing does. Not much has changed in 80 years except that the business world has adopted this same, nonsensical mindset. Most organizations invest the bulk of their training dollars in lecture-and-memorize methods, as if listening to lectures and reading manuals suddenly caused all the information presented to be magically engraved in one's mind, turning novices into experts overnight.

What's particularly galling about this situation is that the computer has made learning-by-doing a realistic option in many situations; computer simulations open up myriad possibilities. One only has to look at the development of the air flight simulator as a training tool to grasp the possibilities.

You would think that organizations desperate to gain the competitive advantage of a highly competent workforce would capitalize on learning-by-doing. A partial reason they miss the boat stems from the reasons detailed in the last chapter. But the cause of their reluctance is also that managers don't understand the virtual learning process and how to implement it. Let's start by viewing the process through the eyes of a child.

HOW KIDS LEARN

I was in a bookstore the other day when a woman pushing a stroller said "excuse me" because I was blocking her path. I moved out of the way and along came a two-year-old toddling behind her. She looked up at me and said "excuse me." Because I was not blocking her way I did nothing. She ran screaming to her mother: "Mommy, I said 'excuse me' but he didn't move." Her mother laughed, which was the correct response. Her daughter will not grow up "excuse-me defective." She will learn what *excuse me* means because she will keep trying and noting what happens.

"Papa carry you," my daughter used to shout, raising her arms to be carried. "Papa carry me," I corrected time and time again. My daughter no longer makes this mistake. It took a while but she got her pronouns right, which leads me to my point: *We accept our children's failures as part of the learning process.*

We don't become hysterical when children make mistakes and try and talk them out of these mistakes. We trust they will eventually learn how to ask for what they need. When you try to tell your two-year-old to do or not to do something—"Don't hit Johnny," "Share your toys with Billy," "Play nice"—there is a good chance your child will ignore your advice. A child learns to share and be nice through experience; Johnny (one hopes) realizes that he has a better time with other kids when he doesn't smack them (and gets smacked back).

Underlying this learning is a goal: to make the world conform to your wishes, to get people to move, to be carried. If you have a goal, you can learn a lot. You're willing to be corrected for your mistakes and accept "try this, do that" advice in order to achieve your goal. Remember, though, that goals only work this way if they're your own rather than someone else's. My daughter learned how to ask to be carried not because her objective was to learn proper English (my goal for her) but because she wanted to be carried. Employees' goals revolve around doing their jobs better (and reaping the personal, financial, and career rewards that accrue to high performers). Unfortunately, most traditional training fails to help people meet their goals.

HOW DO YOU GET TO CARNEGIE HALL?

It's not that the business world abhors learning-by-doing. The lower the skill level, the more likely that a company is training people through some sort of learning-by-doing method. People learn to operate a piece of machinery by looking over an "expert's" shoulder and then trying to do what the expert did. Organizations are usually not so foolish as to try to train forklift operators in the classroom. In cooking schools, instructors use learning-by-doing as the instructional method both because no other way makes sense and because failure isn't catastrophic (unless, of course, you're a gourmet who considers soggy pasta and rubbery squid to be an affront to the senses).

But when it comes to "people" skills—sales, customer service, managerial training, and executive development—companies revert to the school model. They use in-house universities, guest lecturers, elaborate manuals, and tests to impart knowledge. One large bank, for instance, boasts that it offers employees 1000 different courses. Executive development and leadership programs abound. Organizations justify their programs by saying that they inspire the learner; they catalyze new ways of thinking; and they introduce learners to new policies and procedures.

Terrific. I'm all for encouraging people to try new things. But no matter how inspired and enlightened people are, two principles of learning remain:

- Nothing anyone says (no matter how eloquent the speaker or insightful the words) will do any more than inspire you. You must *internalize* procedures to do a better job. To do this you must try them out and receive help when you fail.

- Even if you could learn to do a better job by hearing
  about a marvelous new management technique, it still
  wouldn't matter; if you didn't practice that technique
  over and over again, you wouldn't remember it for
  long.

I can give a child the best instruction money can buy in how
to ride a bicycle. I can show her a step-by-step procedure for getting on the bike and pedaling it; I can show her films that
demonstrate how one keeps one's balance while pedaling; I can
inspire her with stories of bicycling daring do. But unless the
child gets on the bike, gets help when she falls off, and practices
until she doesn't fall again, she's never going to learn how to
ride.

Think about a particular skill of your own job. Did you
master it because of the company's training program or because
of a course you took in business school? Neither. You mastered
that skill through months—no, years—of practice. By gathering
experience and dealing with hundreds of cases, you gradually
learned the subtleties of the job that aren't easily taught. No one
can tell you how to handle a particularly difficult customer; you
can't read a manual about how to manage subordinates fairly
but firmly. You need to jump in and learn what works firsthand.
That's how leaders learn to lead. Reading all those books on
leadership won't do it. Only when you find that your management approach results in low morale and high turnover are you
motivated to be a different, more effective type of leader.

Similarly, when you see that you have inspired your subordinates, when you see their improvement and know you are
partly responsible, you feel secure that you know what you are
doing. Ironically, you may not actually know what you are doing in the sense that you may not be able to clearly state what it
is you just did. But you will become confident in your own intu-
itions about what to do, and that is very important.

When I lecture, I tell my audience that lecturing is silly because "none of you will remember much of what I'm saying." In
a few days or a few weeks, listeners will forget just about everything I told them. The value of lectures—and the value of school

and traditional training—is to get people started in the right direction. It is, in fact, the value of this book. If I'm sufficiently provocative, funny, and insightful—in other words, if I'm entertaining enough so you don't tune me out—I may induce you to think about what I have said (a kind of mental doing) or, even better, to give my ideas a try. But I can't do for you what you need to do yourself. You need to practice, and for that you need practice environments—environments in which people enjoy the freedom to experiment using virtual learning. For instance, managers of a restaurant chain we work for wanted us to train all its managers, so I said, "Fine, let's build a simulated restaurant."

Naturally, that would have been an ambitious undertaking, so the managers responded as many organizations do: "That's so complex and expensive, can't we start with something simple?"

Many organizations want to start "simply." That's not always possible, but let's consider three easy steps you can use to get a feel for the virtual learning process.

GETTING STARTED WITH VIRTUAL LEARNING

Step 1: Think of a Job in Your Organization That Requires Well-Defined, Tangible Skills

When organizations tell me they want to start virtual learning using something simple, I ask them to name a job that's easy to perform. The aforementioned restaurant chain managers told me that would be their hostess jobs. "Anyone can be a hostess," they said. Not true. A common mistake is to choose a position that only seems easy; some jobs that appear simple require complex skills that are difficult to teach. A hostess has to deal with a wide range of human issues—drunks, obnoxious customers, people who become ill, and so on. Though anyone is theoretically qualified to be a hostess, the reality is that doing the job well demands certain intangible skills.

A job that the restaurant chain thought to be much more difficult—that of bartender—is actually much easier from a computer-based training perspective. The restaurant felt that bartending was difficult because there were so many drinks and mixing procedures to memorize. From a computer perspective, though, it's an eminently simple job to simulate. A simulation for a bartender position is relatively fast and inexpensive to build—learning how to make one drink requires the same skills as learning to make another. It is the practice that introduces the complexity.

The point here is that if you want to start simply using virtual learning simulations, pick a job with well-defined, repeatable skills.

Step 2: Figure Out Your Most Pressing Training Issue

Organizations often want to start virtual learning efforts where the hurt is greatest. Some managers arrive at my doorstep in crisis—they're desperate to get people up to speed in some job, procedure, or process and a smart human resources executive recognizes that traditional training won't suffice.

All this panic reaction is fine, as long as you keep the following caveat in mind: Someone in your organization must have already done what you want others to learn to do.

"We want you to teach our people how to work within the great new process we're implementing." As I've stated before (and will state again) this is a common request, and it's one that's very difficult to fulfill. If you lack experts in a given area, you lack the knowledge critical to mastering that area. Who is going to tell you about the tricks of making that process work? Better to get that process up and running before you try to train an entire organization.

The ideal circumstance is when someone comes to the Institute for the Learning Sciences (ILS) and says: "We have someone in our company who can do this job perfectly, she knows how to talk about what it takes to do the job well, and our problem is that we want to create 100 people just like her and we can't do it fast enough."

Step 3: Gather Stories

Why stories? Because that's where golden nuggets of organizational knowledge reside. In every organization, unofficial tips and tricks for outstanding job performance assume shape in stories that lay dormant in each employee's head. These stories are rarely told to other employees who have the exact same job and could benefit greatly from hearing them. I should emphasize that such stories are usually far removed from the job descriptions created by HR departments; those dry documents only *hint* at what's important to learn in language that never inspires, such as "Job X has the following 10 responsibilities. . . ." It's analogous to telling a beginning art student that Monet painted a lot of water lilies in a blurry kind of way. No matter what you say, you can't really learn what Monet is all about until you delve beneath the neutrality of the description.

In the world of work, war stories fill you in on what lies beneath the surface. Unfortunately, these stories are not included in traditional training. Often they are about the unofficial procedures, the things that really get the job done. To hear them, you often need to go for drinks with a bunch of veteran employees or hang around the lunchroom. That's where you'll hear about how Sally needed to meet a number of tight deadlines and devised an ingenious shortcut inspired by a Seinfeld rerun. It's listening to some MIS guy proudly detailing how he ignored his boss's instructions and figured out how to get the most out of a piece of software.

Every organization has thousands of stories. The problem is getting people to tell them. Sometimes the problem is that organizations are so large and spread out, people never get a chance to meet other employees who could tell them relevant stories. It's also possible that people are reluctant to tell their stories because they make them, the organization, or their bosses look bad. Or it may be that some people aren't good storytellers.

As a result, designers of virtual learning packages have to be clever to draw these stories out. Sometimes the interviewer can get someone started by asking, "Do you have a story about working here that you wish everyone in the company knew?" Institute designers often catalyze storytelling with a number of specific, leading questions, such as:

- What was the most interesting thing that's happened to you on the job?

- What do you like about your job?
- What about your job is hard to do?
- What difficult problem did you solve yourself?
- Did you ever have a time when . . . (such as, someone wouldn't let you do X or tried to get you to do Y)?

Once interviewers hit upon a promising response, they should become more specific in their questioning, trying to draw out stories about screw-ups, complexities, and crazy situations. Later you'll get more specific ideas to help you ask questions that elicit usable stories from your people.

There are different ways to use these stories for learning, including creating "corporate memories"—collections of stories told by company experts easily accessed through computer systems. But for now, let's focus on turning these stories into learning tools, or simulations. I'm not going to get into the actual process, concentrating instead on the outcomes—the ingredients that are crucial for effective simulations.

LEARNING CAN BE SIMULATING

Like a good novel, a good simulation asks your learners to suspend their disbelief. Whether you're creating a simulation on a computer or through role-playing, you want participants to experience the event as if it were really happening. Perhaps more to the point, you want to avoid evoking an unnatural response—a response someone wouldn't give in real life.

We've created all types of simulations for our clients—here's a sampling:

- Boston Chicken—trainees practice ringing up orders on a simulated cash register in order to become faster and more accurate, helped by an online tutor.
- Ameritech—newly hired account executives learn how to sell *Yellow Pages* advertising in typical selling situations, helped by videotapes of experts and other learning tools to meet challenging situations.

- Andersen Consulting—for new Andersen managers, this system simulates the performance evaluation process to impart supervisory skills.

These simulations are guided by the stories we've been told. From those stories we create scripts that place trainees in situations that feel authentic. They're designed and filmed so that people naturally make the mistakes they would in real work situations. When those mistakes occur, all sorts of things can happen. An actor playing the role of the boss can criticize you for doing something wrong. An associate can come into the room and inform you that the employee you just fired has filed a discrimination lawsuit against the company. You might lose a major customer because you neglected to meet their delivery deadline.

These scenarios pack a punch. When learners goof up, they don't feel like this was just a computer exercise. It feels real. When failure occurs, the simulation is often designed to give users a number of options on how to proceed. A menu of choices appears, and users can opt for hearing an expert tell a story related to their failure. Learners may want to try the scenario over again. They may determine it would be helpful to do some research. Users may choose to call upon a coach to give them some advice. CD-ROM technology makes it possible to have these choices and to access everything from text to animation to video clips. It also makes it possible for the people in the scenario to react to the user's statements and decisions in a realistic manner. If users are rude to a customer, for instance, she'll react with the invective the learners deserve for being bozos. Sophisticated systems also make it possible for trainees to navigate their way through a scenario in different ways. One person may move through it more slowly than another learner. One person may prefer to ask the coach a lot of questions, whereas another just wants to keep going through the scenario until he gets it right. The simulations accommodate a variety of personality types and preferences.

Verisimilitude is created in many ways. Perhaps one of the most surprising ways—at least surprising to people schooled in right and wrong answers—is the ambiguity we've built into our programs. In a simulation ILS did for the Environmental

Protection Agency, for instance, users are receiving a call from someone who complains that the ground is polluted in their area. An expert pops up on the screen and advises that if the learners don't feel the call is serious or significant—and if they're very busy—they should move on to other things. Another expert, however, advises that users treat callers like their friends and attempt to work with them.

In other words, the program communicates that there's not always one right answer. It invites trainees to learn to use their own judgment rather than rely on someone else's—especially when the someone else isn't as close to the situation as you are. Organizations today are facing increasingly complex situations where there are many possible answers. Traditional training that insists on right and wrong answers disempowers the individual—it robs people of their decision-making ability. That's not to say that simulations should always create ambiguous situations, since there are times when right and wrong options clearly exist. In a program we created for a British water utility, the simulation communicated that it was wrong to frighten customers about possible pollution in their drinking water. We communicate this information only after the trainee actually does something like this. Then we use a story that tells about a time when a customer service person actually panicked a customer who then called the police and the health department and made things quite difficult for the company.

Sometimes simulations, like real life, need to throw some curves. In an EPA program designed to teach people to run public meetings, we had a priest appear at the simulated meeting and complain about sanitation in a poor neighborhood. Since the trainee was expecting a discussion of other issues, he had to learn to refocus the meeting on a very serious problem. Dealing with the unexpected is a critical skill in a rapidly-changing world, and it's a skill most training programs ignore.

HELPING PEOPLE LEARN TO DO JUST ABOUT ANYTHING

The cynic might scoff that although it is possible to simulate simple situations, it's impossible to simulate complex ones. It's certainly easier to teach a simple skill (pounding a nail into a board) than one that impacts judgment and attitude (how to develop partnerships with customers). For that matter, it's easier to teach people to do 10 things rather than 100. Despite this, our teams have found that simulations are effective in helping people learn to deal with change, take risks, value diversity, and many other amorphous skills. But they're only effective if designers are clever about constructing the simulations.

For example, let's say you want people to learn to be less re-sistant to change. If designers create a program that telegraphs the punch—that sets up a situation in which it's obvious users are supposed to be scared by change—people will respond as re-quested and not learn anything. Trainees easily fall into "stu-dent-mode," parroting behavior that they know is wanted by the teacher. If, however, the designer builds a situation that causes them to act naturally—to resist change reflexively—then the designer has produced the ideal simulation for learning. When people resist change unconsciously, the program points out their resistance to them, catching them off guard.

This enlightenment can be accomplished through comput-ers or through role-playing. The former has the following five advantages:

- It's cheaper over time.
- It allows for failure without embarrassment.
- Do it once and it can be used many times.
- The same things happen each time.
- World-class experts can be the teachers if they have been videotaped.

Live simulations have their advantages as well:

- They are cheaper initially.
- They seem more realistic.
- They are replicable.
- Different things happen each time.
- World-class experts can be the teachers if they are there.

In terms of making an impact using live simulations, it's crucial to have the right people playing the right roles. You may have
experienced a role-playing scenario in which a facilitator points
to one trainee and says, "You be the CEO" and points to another
trainee and says "You be his subordinate." Then these same two
people play out the same scenario by switching roles. The problem, of course, is that neither person knows how to be a CEO—
each is about as credible as Jerry Lewis playing Hamlet. When a
simulation calls for a CEO, trainers should go out and recruit ex-
CEOs to play the role. In fact, ILS was doing a simulation for
Diamond Technologies in which the ex-CEO playing the chief executive role fired the consulting firm and shut down the simulation. This wasn't expected; everyone was a bit taken aback when
it happened. But it was a great learning experience for the participants. As the ex-CEO said, "When I was heading a company and
a consulting firm did what they did, I terminated the relationship.
So it seemed that the people who were being trained should
know that."

This type of simulation on a computer would never match
the impact of the ex-CEO's spontaneous reaction. In another instance, we were creating a computer simulation designed to
teach employees not to discriminate, and some people suggested incorporating a sexy woman and seeing if any male employees favored her over other customers. Of course, a sexy
woman on a computer screen is not quite the same as a sexy
woman in real life, making it much easier to mimic the "correct"
behavior.

The problems with live simulations, however, should be
taken into consideration. For one thing, these simulations pose
logistical difficulties. Trainers can't train hundreds of employees
simultaneously—trainers have to put on a lot of performances in
a lot of locations, and it's difficult to assemble all the role-players
for each performance. Perhaps more importantly, participants
are more likely to avoid failure in role-playing situations than in
computer simulations. It's embarrassing to fail while others are
watching, and so their behavior is shaped by this fear of embar-

rassing themselves. They don't understand that they must fail in order to learn.

Because computer simulations are private, people are much more willing to fail, and this fact tends to give computer simulations an edge over role-playing. Technological advances also make these simulations a great deal of fun, and learning flourishes in a fun environment. The portability of software is also a consideration—people can learn any time, any place.

And there are times when trainers can combine simulations with role-playing, capitalizing on the best of both worlds.

Whether the simulation is live or computerized, virtual learning won't work if the people lack motivation. The simulation must help them achieve a goal they want to achieve. It's why this book often refers to simulations as *goal-based scenarios*. Think about this concept in terms of how children learn. Kids want to learn to ride bikes, and that motivates them to practice and fail until they achieve that goal. But do they want to learn the names of cities throughout the world? Probably not. But designers can create a computer simulation where the goal is to win a game by traveling to various cities for some purpose, and suddenly users learn because they need to do so in order to achieve a goal that they want to achieve.

ILS created a simulation for a company designed to help them deal with a certain type of customer. Although the simulation was for recent hires, a number of veteran employees asked to participate in the simulation. Why? Because they were eager to learn something that would help them perform their jobs better. There were cases in the simulation that they had never encountered and they were worried about the right way to handle them.

No doubt there are some employees who don't care about how they perform—some who are lazy, cynical, and just putting in time—and who lack the motivation to learn. But our experience tells us that the majority of employees want to do well and hate the feeling of incompetence. Few things are more frustrating than not being able to do a job effectively because you lack skills and knowledge you know you should have.

WHO ARE THE BEST CANDIDATES FOR VIRTUAL LEARNING?

Everyone. There should be CEO-training courses, though the common view of CEOs as godlike figures makes it difficult for them to admit that they could learn a thing or two. In fact, it's always struck me as ironic that companies won't let low-level people learn on the job and insist they be trained but we're content to let high-level people learn while they work without the benefit of training.

As painful as it might be to admit, no one knows automatically how to do his or her job. It's difficult for corporate managers to acknowledge that their organizations are constantly hiring people for jobs they don't know how to do. How could they? Although people come to jobs with certain skills—public relations, legal, MIS, and other types of expertise—they lack understanding of the job's unique aspects.

I once hired a chief operations officer, a former president of a software firm. Although his experience indicated he was a good candidate for the job, he was far from an expert at this particular job. He didn't know much about my company's historical dealings with clients; he didn't understand my attitudes about different policies and procedures; he couldn't have known about how to get the most out of the particular people who would be working for him. As terrific as his generic management skills were, he had a lot of specifics to learn. High-level executives need training too. They too need to learn from experts and learn from failure.

There's nothing wrong with this. The sooner we acknowledge this reality, the easier it will be to broaden the scope of the staff who benefit from virtual learning.

3

CHAPTER

FAILURE:

The Engine That Powers Virtual Learning

The F word (*failure*) is anathema to both teachers and CEOs. We punish students with bad grades when they offer the wrong answers on tests. We punish employees with negative performance reviews when they make mistakes. The bigger the failure, the bigger the punishment: Flunking and termination await those who fail frequently.

All of these negative consequences give failure a bad name, which is too bad because people need to fail in order to learn. As Chapter 2 illustrated, simulations offer people two possible ways of responding to failure:

- I don't know why I'm screwing up, help me.
- I know I'm screwing up but I'll figure out what's going wrong myself.

Either response is fine. The participant's learning style dictates which response he or she chooses in a given instance. The point is that all simulations designed by LSC offer people opportunities to fail and opportunities to consider why they failed.

In a sense, the programs are simulating the natural learning process. Again, remember how kids learn. When they want something from mom or dad, toddlers will scream or hit their parents to get attention. When children start dressing themselves, they put on their pants backwards. When they begin to talk, they say, "I goed to my room." Small children are failure machines, failing hundreds of thousands of times before they learn the proper way to get parents' attention, dress, and speak.

For adults, failure can take many forms. The first day on the job, the boss tells the employee to get to work, and the new hire's natural response is, "How?" It's a failure in the sense that the new employee doesn't know how to do the job properly and has to keep asking for help to understand what to do next. Professors, like most people, are completely lost the first year on the job. All they know is their area of study. New professors don't know how to deal with the mind-boggling array of questions students ask: "What should I major in?"; "Do you think this internship will help get me into graduate school?"; "What courses should I take?" Most neophyte professors fail to answer these questions effectively.

Failure can also translate into an inability to predict the outcome of behavior. A marketing analyst fails to realize that her lack of knowledge about an emerging market resulted in a lost opportunity for her company. On a larger scale, military and political leaders of the United States were unable to predict what would happen when the country became involved in Vietnam. Certainly U.S. leaders learned from this failure, because every time Congress considers intervening militarily overseas, they're reminded of the Vietnam failure.

Given the many ways failure can be defined, let's focus on the definition relevant to learning.

EXPECTATION FAILURE

Failure means to mess up, to fall short of a goal, to strike out, to break down, to lose. Lots of synonyms exist, but from a learning perspective, they lack one key modifier. For learning to take place, there has to be *expectation failure*. In other words, an employee expects to make a sale but it falls through; he expects a new process to save money but it doesn't; he expects to meet a deadline but misses the target date. In one sense, expectation failure has a broader scope because it can encompass positive experiences: An investor purchased a stock thinking it might go up a few points, but she didn't expect it to skyrocket 50 points in a matter of days. This might look like success, but it's a failure because she didn't expect it, can't explain it, and doesn't understand it.

What does all this have to do with learning? Consider what happens when learners' expectations are met. For instance, when they sit down to work at their desks they always manage to land in their chairs. Because their expectations are met, they don't have to think about or explain sitting down. But what would happen if one day they sat down and landed on the floor, missing the chair? They would have to think about and explain this failure. These outcomes lead to two guiding principles of failure:

- Real thinking never starts until the learner fails.
- It is easy to recognize their expectation failures because people insist on explaining them.

Thinking and explaining catalyze learning. People who go through life repeating the same successful behavior, never trying anything new or different (at which they're bound to fail) learn precious little. Most of us don't have that problem. In a work environment, the vast majority of employees experience a constant state of constant expectation failure, the only possible exceptions being those at the very bottom of the ladder. These people are often forced into routines, doing the same job the same way year in and year out. They hate their jobs. This leads to a curious point. In an odd way, expectation failure is fun; it makes life interesting.

Most people are swimming about in a sea of failure. You might think that they'd drown in our unrealized expectations. Discouraged and dismayed, they would simply give up and sink from sight (or furious and frustrated, quit or do something to get themselves fired). In fact, most people work well in an environment of failure. They're able to do so because their mental life depends on expectation failure—it is the natural way their minds function.

THAT REMINDS ME OF A STORY

When people experience expectation failure, their minds create a reminding strategy. It takes that failure, gives it a name, stores it away and retrieves it when they fail again in exactly the same way. This reminding strategy enables people to think about that old failure within the context of the new failure. This isn't done consciously; it's a natural mechanism that helps people cope with failure.

A personal experience will illustrate this process. A friend of mine requested my advice about which woman he should marry. He said that he loved one woman and she loved him, but added that he thought she was crazy. He didn't love the second woman as much but explained that she wasn't as crazy and he thought she'd be a good mother.

"Let me tell you a story," I responded. Something my friend said triggered a story I had labeled in my mind, a story revolving around a failure I had made in making a selection decision. A number of years ago, I had decided to hire a CEO to run my company so I could devote more time to being a professor. I interviewed someone who seemed eminently qualified for the job, and our interview went well. During the course of that interview, the candidate mentioned how he'd been going through a divorce and boasted about winning a heated custody battle that entitled him to both the kids and the house. I hired him, but a few years later we had a falling out over the fact that when he was placed in a difficult situation, he became vicious. His behavior was similar to his boastful description of his custody victory, I realized with hindsight.

To my friend who was trying to decide between the two women I said, "Listen to what people tell you about themselves, because they mean it."

Now think about how I "found" this story to tell. The process my unconscious mind went through must have looked something like this:

1. I asked myself, "How do you predict people's behavior when they're telling you something bad about themselves?"
2. My failure to predict my former CEO's behavior became a labeled memory in my head.
3. My friend communicates that he is trying to predict the behavior of a person whom he suspects might behave badly.
4. The words of my friend trigger the labeled memory in my head, and I tell my story.

Now apply the point of this anecdote to learning. As people make mistakes and experience trouble, it would be nice to be reminded of all the right stories at the right times to help deal with the problems. Sometimes, this is exactly what happens. When it happens in a work situation, that reminding becomes expertise: Employees say to themselves, "I had that problem before; here's the solution."

But sometimes people lack the experiences to summon up stories they can learn from. To obtain those experiences and turn them into reminding stories, people need to fail on the job or in a simulation. Gaining expertise through simulations is a more practical alternative for most organizations.

WHY NOT A SUCCESS-BASED LEARNING SYSTEM?

A success-focused system would tell people what the right procedures and policies are, get employees to memorize them, and have the learners repeat the solutions. People would try to be successful at their jobs by imitating others who have been successful in the past. The premise is that if the learner studies someone else's success, the learner can copy it.

The Results of Success

When I was an advisor at Yale, an ambitious freshman approached me and asked me to tell him what courses he should take—at the time Yale didn't have any requirements. I advised him to take whatever interested him. "No," he protested, "I want to take the ones that will help me do well in my career. What courses did *you* take?" I listed the required courses that I was forced to sign up for years ago. "Okay," he said, "I'll take those, because if they made you successful, they'll make me successful."

Of course, those courses didn't make me successful. Yet the myth of success is powerful, and it seduces us into believing we need to avoid failure at all costs. In reality, people who never fail are bored out of their skulls and lack risk-taking ability and creativity. They can do one job competently in one specific way—for them, learning is a closed-end process that doesn't allow for flexibility. Organizations may gain employees who can complete simple tasks effectively, but they lose the innovation and adaptability necessary to compete in a global marketplace; they may also lose employees who are bored with their success and leave for greater challenges elsewhere.

Learning from Exceptions

Just as important, a success-based system doesn't allow for variations. Failure-based systems prepare people to deal with situations where things don't go according to plan. When I consulted for an Italian railway company, managers told me about a recent accident involving one of their trains. The company had just added on some new cars that were larger than the norm. The computer that tracked the routes for the drivers gave an all clear signal because it had used the old measure for the cars. The driver of a passing train got the all clear. He relied on what he had been told by the computer. These larger cars' size caused them to stick out past a station platform, and an accident ensued. Following the railway company's procedures, the driver was watching his computer screen, which failed to alert him that an accident was about to happen. If the driver had looked out his window, he would have seen the problem and been able to prevent it. No doubt, this driver will be alert to this problem in the future, failure being the good teacher that it is.

But what about other drivers? And what about other situations where the rules aren't applicable?

The railroad company needs to build a simulation in which engineers experience exceptions to the rules, where they fail to deal effectively with problems using traditional responses. Given a chance to practice failing, engineers will learn what to do when things don't go according to plan.

FAILING WITH DIGNITY

Most kids don't mind failing until they start school. As long as parents tolerate mistakes with good humor, children are perfectly willing to mess up time and again. All this changes when school begins and their failures become the subject of public ridicule—grades are posted for everyone to see or a teacher chastises a student who does poorly in front of the entire class. The same thing happens in organizations when people who have made mistakes or taken risks that didn't pan out receive public tongue-lashings from the boss. This creates an environment where it's difficult to learn from failure—rather than admitting an error and seeking help, employees prefer to cover it up and avoid public humiliation.

Computer simulations work so well because they enable users to fail in private. Ameritech has a standard classroom course designed to help people develop telephone skills. ILS created a computer simulation designed to do the same thing. Employees overwhelmingly preferred the computer simulation to the classroom. People commented that they were "embarrassed" to give the wrong answer in the classroom and were "afraid to take a chance." In private, they felt much more comfortable with taking chances and making mistakes.

These feelings arise because failure should be a private experience in which a learner has the opportunity to reflect and think about other options not chosen. The computer doesn't care when someone makes a mistake; it creates an environment well-suited to reflecting on one's mistakes.

This desire for privacy for our mistakes doesn't mean that managers have to treat employees with kid gloves. It's fine for

bosses to communicate their disapproval when people do something wrong, as long as the disapproval is related to goals.

REAL GOALS MOTIVATE LEARNING FROM FAILURE

Savvy managers recognize that seeking approval from the boss
is a common employee goal. These managers use this goal in a
variety of ways to motivate people to learn. Managers use everything from sarcasm to warnings to communicate that they're not
happy with their subordinates' work, and that to make them
happy they'll have to figure out what went wrong and ask for
help if necessary. As long as managers don't humiliate their employees in front of others, no harm will be done.

Many training approaches assume that people naturally
have the goal to learn: Build the training and they will come. But
if you've ever seen what happens when a teacher leaves a classroom or a boss leaves a meeting, you know that isn't always so.
People have the goal of gossiping, of taking coffee breaks and of
making personal phone calls. They have other, nobler goals, but
you have to recognize what they are and link them to learning.
Otherwise people will fail and learn nothing.

Failure, in and of itself, isn't a catalyst. Every manager has
seen employees who have made major mistakes become apathetic or despondent. If people are not motivated by a goal,
they'll get stuck in failure. To catalyze the self-explaining
process that leads people out of failure, they need motivation. If
it's there, they'll ask themselves the following three questions:

- How did I fail?
- How can I fix this?
- What do I have in my experience to help me?

Some employees, because of their particular learning styles,
won't self-explain. They'll fail and start to feel frustrated. To prevent this from happening, LSC's simulation displays always include a "Why?" button. Users click it and are told stories by
people who have failed in similar ways. Instead of feeling frustrated, people feel comforted to learn they're not the only ones to

have failed and then continue the simulation, attempting to meet their goals.

Perceptive managers recognize the goals to which their people will respond. The goals may be obvious and financially-related: promotions, raises, and bonuses. The goals may have to do with the approval of a boss or one's peers. They may revolve around winning a competition or achieving a performance target. Whatever the goals, they need to be incorporated into learning systems or else people won't have the energy to figure out their failures.

THE PARADOX OF REAL GOALS AND "UNREAL" SIMULATIONS

What motivates employees to learn in simulations when the learners know their failure has no impact in the real world of their organizations? There are a number of answers to that question. First, think of that pilot-in-training at the controls of a flight simulator. He makes a maneuver and is informed that if he were to do that same maneuver in a real plane, he would have killed himself and 148 passengers. The goal of keeping oneself and one's passengers alive would motivate most people to learn from this failure.

But consider a less dramatic situation. A team at LSC created a computer simulation for Anixter Corp. in which salespeople arranged a meeting with customers to sell them the company's services. One of the first tasks was to make a phone call to a customer. If the learner didn't make an effective call, he or she didn't get the appointment. If the learner failed to invite the right person to accompany the learner to the meeting, he or she had to start the whole process over again. These and other situations tap into common employee goals—the desire to do well in the simulation, the need to know how to deal with difficult situations that will arise in the field.

Suspending Your Disbelief

Ensuing chapters describe simulations in more detail and you'll get a better sense of how compelling and involving they are. For the moment, however, think of a sophisticated CD-ROM game. Playing it, you may wander around a completely unreal landscape or extricate yourself from a castle's maze. These worlds don't exist in real life, yet many people describe being afraid as they wander the spooky house displayed by the CD-ROM or being angry and frustrated when they make a mistake in solving an adventure game puzzle. The reason people feel that way is because the CD-ROM is so well made that players suspend their disbelief and enter into the virtual reality of the disk's world. When CD-ROM simulations are well made, failures are immediately familiar and believable to trainees; they "feel" exactly like ones trainees might make while doing their real jobs.

In a simulation for Target, for instance, an irritating customer attempting to return merchandise evokes the same frustration that certain customers evoke in real life. The scene isn't scripted and acted randomly; it was shaped from stories told by Target employees in the attempt to capture the specific details—the lack of a receipt, the customer becoming more confrontational when he hears that he is past the date when store policy allows him to return merchandise. The designers built the scene to the point that trainees frequently fail without thinking. They scream at the customer or they robotically recite store policy. The difference between it and a real life situation is that the simulation stops at this failure point and helps trainees understand why they failed and what their options are. The employees are motivated to learn because just about everyone feels uncomfortable in these situations; employees want to know what alternatives they have to citing store policy or engaging in a shouting match with customers.

Approval of Peers as a Motivator

In live simulations, people are not motivated as much by approval of the trainers as they are by approval of their peers in the room. If designers create a simulated business unit as part of the scenario, for instance, most people in that unit want to do their jobs well—they're acutely aware of how others in the unit view them. It's therefore important to find a way to harness the power of that goal to help everyone learn from the mistakes they'll inevitably make.

I don't pretend to believe that simulations always prepare people to handle real situations effectively. There can be problems in applying solutions from one environment to another, especially if the user is relatively inexperienced in a given area. If, for instance, she is a young manager who has gone through a few simulations on decision making, she shouldn't expect to make all types of major, complex decisions effectively. Still, the "reminding" concept presented earlier in the chapter holds true. If a simulation is done well, it seems real and becomes a labeled memory that's triggered by a similar experience—she is reminded of it despite the fact that it's a simulation. A failure is a failure, and whether it occurs in a simulation or a work situation, the experience helps the user learn.

4 CHAPTER

RULES TO LEARN BY

As early chapters have explained, stories, simulations, goals, practice, fun, and failure are all critical to real learning. Does that mean I expect all readers to change their training immediately and wholeheartedly embrace these principles? Of course not. Experience, as they say, is the best teacher. Until your experiences bring the points in this book to life, all this book can do is get you thinking in a new direction. The odds are that new direction runs counter to what you've been taught in school and in business. It's not easy to reject years and years of propaganda.

THE RULES

To help readers reject the old precepts, I'd like to do two things. The next chapter provides a glimpse of an organization that is revolutionizing the way its people learn. But here are 10 "rules" that can guide companies' thinking and training. They're not rules as much as thought-starters and misconception-breakers for people willing to fail in order to learn.

1. People Remember Best What They Feel the Most

It is difficult to forget the first person who broke your heart or the car accident that broke your body. Intense feelings stick with people; anything that packs an emotional or visceral punch imprints itself on their minds. That's why dry, boring, lifeless manuals and lectures are instantly forgettable. It takes the emotional intensity of experience—or a simulation of that experience—for stories to stick.

Which brings to mind sex education. Some of you may recall the old Monty Python routine in which John Cleese is teaching a sex education class by making love to his wife. Contrary to what you might expect, the students aren't paying attention. Instead they're dozing, throwing spitballs, talking among themselves, and generally ignoring Cleese and his wife. The lesson here is that even something intrinsically interesting can become dull if it is treated as a subject the learner has to learn and if it lacks personal meaning. There's not much emotion in watching someone else have an experience (and even prurient interest can be killed if it's "required for the test").

In business, people remember highly emotional encounters: the time they blew an important business deal, being chewed out by the boss, or finding out a project was being shut down after six months of hard work. Although it's true that simulations don't have the same impact as real work situations, they can engender strong feelings. Crashing a simulated plane can be quite frightening. The point here is that role-playing or computer simulations should attempt to evoke emotion rather than be purely cognitive exercises.

2. Dumb Employees Aren't Born; They're Made

Organizations are constantly selling their people short. How many times have you heard someone say, "We have to simplify the training because we hire idiots" or some variation on that theme? Certainly people do act like idiots at work, but only because they've been trained to act that way. A reporter in Chicago wrote a travel series in which he drove a rented car through 48 states. After racking up over 17,000 miles, he returned the car to the rental company, and the first and only question the service representative asked was, "Did you put in gas?" Now that's an idiotic question given the mileage, but it's the one that all the rental car company employees are trained to ask. It's as if organizations assume that their low-level people are only capable of memorizing five questions.

When I go to an airline counter, I sometimes ask, "Is the plane on time?", and the airline rep usually looks up at the board and says yes. Then I ask whether the incoming plane actually landed. That's when the rep is forced to find out the real answer to the question. These people are trained to look at the listing on the board because airlines don't believe their people can deal with the complex issues of why planes are late.

What companies don't understand is that even people with low IQs or those who did poorly in school are good learners; they usually have a natural impulse to help others and meet customers' needs. That impulse is drummed out of people by companies that say, "Memorize these responses and follow the rules." There's tremendous stress when people have to act in a way that they know isn't helpful, and stress makes employees cynical and apathetic and drives them to quit.

Train these people by simulating situations they're likely to encounter, let them make mistakes trying to be helpful, and they'll eventually accumulate sufficient experiences to be effective in a wide variety of customer interactions.

3. Deliver Training Just in Time (Or When a Learner Has Just Failed and Really Needs Help)

This is difficult for organizations to do because they're locked into training schedules. One hundred employees learn about a new sales tool over the course of a week; that's when a facility and the trainers are available to teach that tool. But those 100 employees will need the sales vehicle at different times—some may need it three weeks after the course, some may need it three years later. Distance learning has become popular because it employs neat high-tech gadgetry and is financially expedient—it can train thousands of people all over the world simultaneously—a wonderful thing for a global organization. The problem is, the more people learning at the same time, the more people whose questions aren't answered. For a lesson to really sink in, the trainee needs to be failing and asking for help. Trainers need people actively asking questions rather than passively watching "educational" television. Distance learning really is a way to put a lot of distance between the conveyance of information and the time people really need it.

The Learning Sciences Corporation created a learning system for a shipping company that enables users to get guidance when they are engaged in a process. The shipping company has a manual that everyone has read and that contains exactly what employees need to help them when they are doing their jobs, but they don't read it while they are doing their jobs. The information doesn't come to mind if users read the manual months or years ago; it has to be delivered just in time.

4. You Can Fail to Learn Just About Anything

Simulations and role-playing can be used to help people learn soft (people-oriented) skills, not just hard (widget-oriented) ones. Organizations are especially intent on teaching their people soft skills such as leadership, teamwork, and creativity, but they're doing so in ways that range from faddish to foolish.

Many executive development programs have an "adventure" component where teams of executives are challenged to work together to raft whitewater rivers and climb mountains. The assumption is that these activities will help people acquire leadership and team-building skills. What they actually do is help people learn how to raft and climb. If trainers want people to learn to be leaders in a business situation, the trainers have to put them in business leadership situations. Quarterbacks, who are typically great leaders, don't necessarily know how to lead a project through to completion on time and under budget. To teach a skill one must teach it within a relevant context. Simulating business situations can teach leadership and decision making, because so much of leadership is cerebral.

Categorizing and collecting stories about tough decisions leaders have had to make is a good start. Then simulations can be created where people are confronted with some tough (and realistic) decisions: Should I fire five of my senior people who haven't been performing up to snuff or should I spend a good deal of time and money training them to perform better? When faced with these tough decisions, people are ready to hear how experts in leadership resolved similar issues. Even with the help of experts, it's likely that trainees will fail to make the right decisions at first. Leadership is not a simple skill, and the right leadership decision for one won't be the right decision for someone else—personality type will influence decision making, and one person will lead humanistically whereas another will lead charismatically. Still, it's fine to let the trainees fail and obtain an instructive memory for later use.

Companies are also making mistakes when it comes to teaching creativity. Perhaps the biggest one is assuming that people are naturally uncreative. This assumption leads to the development of all sorts of unusual tools and techniques designed to help people become creative—free association, lateral thinking, and so on. None of these tools, however, will overcome the real obstacle to creativity: Negativity. In school and at work, people are constantly told that their ideas are bad. Teachers ridicule kids who make oddball suggestions (because they're not the right answers) and bosses reject ideas that they deem weird, risky, or at odds with traditional practices. All this stifles creativity. Such negativity is too bad, because people are all naturally creative.

Humans live in a constant state of creativity, if it is defined as producing something that no one has produced before. Just forming a sentence or trying to understand a joke is a creative act. Every day people have hundreds of original thoughts and make hundreds of original statements; all sorts of unique ideas about how to do a job better flow through people's minds. Employees don't articulate them because they've been conditioned to believe that the reward for doing so is criticism and ridicule.

In fact, the few people who are considered "creative types" in organizations may be no more creative than their fellow employees; they're often just the ones with the thickest skins. Perhaps 99 out of 100 of their ideas are mediocre, but the creative types have the emotional armor to keep articulating them until a good one pops up.

Given this negativity, the way to help people use their natural creativity is to enable them to practice being creative. Simulations that invite people to formulate original conclusions and that don't make them feel stupid if they're not feasible will enable creative thinking to emerge.

5. Learners Will Teach Themselves Better Than the World's Best Trainer or Highest-Paid Motivational Speaker

Teachers tend to think that they are more important to the learning process than they actually are. People naturally teach themselves. When something goes wrong, people automatically ask themselves how they messed up and seek advice in order not to repeat the same mistake. This is especially true when they're learning complex tasks. When I started my first company (a complex task if ever there was one), I made hundreds of mistakes I would never make again. But I would have made those mistakes no matter how many books I read about how to start a company or how many consultants I asked for advice. Like everyone else, I had to learn the hard way. For instance, when I began it seemed like we had great cash resources and didn't have any money worries. Only the visceral experience of seeing how quickly money disappeared helped me learn a lesson about cashflow and budgeting.

Similarly, I started out wanting to be Mr. Nice Guy and never fire anyone. Most neophyte business owners tell the same story—how they changed from CEOs who tried to be nice to all their employees to bosses who fired people without compunction. What business owners learn with experience is that allowing nonperformers to slide by hurts everyone else in the company; that being a nice guy toward one person who doesn't deserve it hurts all the other hard-working employees who deserve your consideration.

Can someone learn this lesson through a computer simulation or role-playing scenario? An ILS team actually built a program for a client's human resources department designed to teach HR people how to fire employees. Although the program can't possibly duplicate the emotional impact of firing another human being, it does contribute to the accumulation of experiences that is a part of learning. At the least, such simulations help people learn faster and deal with certain issues better.

6. Memorization Without Corresponding Experience Is Worthless

People waste enormous amounts of time attempting to memorize facts, procedures, and slogans. Such memorization has no impact on behavior; it doesn't translate into learned skills. Yet companies persist in forcing their people to commit the 10 principles of quality to memory or studying a list of hiring procedures until they have it down cold. Again, all this goes back to our educational system, which assumes that committing something to memory is learning.

Recall Nancy Reagan's "Just Say No" antidrug campaign and consider why such efforts are futile. As well-intentioned as the campaign was, plastering the slogan over the media didn't change anyone's behavior. The fact that millions of Americans had the slogan branded in their consciousness didn't stop them from using drugs.

Andersen Consulting has the right approach to memorization. Firm believers in Steven Covey's Seven Habits of Highly Effective People, managers wanted their people to commit the habits to memory. An employee can barely turn around in Andersen's offices without bumping into one of the habits—they're on screensavers and walls. Yet Andersen also requested that ILS create simulations that reinforced these Seven Habits. For instance, one of Covey's habits is "First Things First."

ILS's simulation placed Andersen's people in different situations in which they had to juggle a number of goals and priorities and make a decision about what was most important. The designers structured the simulations so participants really had to struggle with prioritizing. For instance, one scenario set the stage so that Andersen employees had to choose between family and job—spend too much time at one and they would lose the other. Failure was inevitable no matter what thing they put first (assuming people consider the loss of a job or a family a failure), but it gave the participants experience in prioritizing tough issues.

Memorizing procedures is often a waste of time, as anyone who drives a car or throws a football understands. After driving for a period of time, a driver doesn't have to think consciously about procedure one, turning the ignition; procedure two, putting the car in drive; procedure three, stepping on the gas pedal so it's depressed a half an inch; and so on.

Someone once asked me whether you should spin a football when you throw it. I used to be a pretty good quarterback and must have thrown thousands of passes, yet I had no idea how to answer the question. I had to actually throw the football and observe whether I rotated the ball as I released it. My expertise was unconscious.

Learning procedures at work follows the same unconscious route. Novices need to practice, make mistakes, practice, and make more mistakes until at some point employees master the procedures and don't have to think about them anymore. All learners memorize when they study training manuals are words. When learners do something repeatedly, they memorize actions.

7. When a Company Buys a Learning System, It Should Come with All the Options

Do various people learn differently? In other words, does it make sense to design a learning experience one way for John and a different way for Mary? Not really. Contrary to common belief, people don't have different learning styles. They do, however, have different personalities. The distinction is important, because we need to be clear that everyone learns the same way. In other words, all people learn through failure and practice, no matter what type of personalities they possess. Designing a learning process different ways for different people is nonsensical (though a trap that some organizations fall into).

On the other hand, it makes sense to take personality differences into account in designing a system. Our software includes various buttons to push: "Now what?," "Why?," "How?," and others. LSC's simulations give people options, recognizing that one individual will be confident and willing to try anything whereas another will be cautious and want to know reasons for taking a step. Any good teacher recognizes that some students need to be coaxed whereas others need to be prodded. A system with options for learning is far more effective than one lacking them.

8. Training Should Open with a Bang

Most employees react to training in one of two ways: Either learners hate it or they look at it as time off from their real jobs. This means that even if you have a good learning system it might not do much good because of your resistance or disinterested audience.

The best way to break through resistance and apathy is with an opening that's immediately involving and fun. This is not a natural training instinct. Most courses begin with a long and boring introduction about why you'll learn what you'll learn. Before the trainer gets to the good stuff, he or she has lost the audience. In virtual learning, training starts by having people do something. Even if they don't understand exactly what they're doing, it's okay as long as they understand they can ask for help as they go along.

9. Trainees Should Be Learning from the World's Best

In reality, training participants are probably learning from "experts" with marginal or mediocre skills. An organization is lucky if it has a handful of real experts—men and women who are among the best at what they do. Because of the size of most companies, it's impossible for everyone to apprentice with the masters. In addition, these experts retire, quit, or die, robbing the organization of their expertise.

A computer simulation offers companies the chance to preserve this expertise. Capturing and integrating expert knowledge into the computer simulation is something every company can do. If the company lack experts in a given area, trainers can find them and film them wherever they are and make their expertise part of the interactive training. Capturing corporate memory in an easily navigable system is important in the age of global, fast-changing companies. Companies need to be able to access their experts on demand whether these masters are in Kuala Lumpur or no longer with the firm at all.

Unfortunately, most companies don't capitalize on expertise. Instead, managers bring in the world's best experts to lecture. As entertaining as this might be and as useful as thought-starters, lecturing doesn't help novices do their jobs better.

10. It's Better to Train the Many Rather Than the Few

In the early days of artificial intelligence (AI), the concept was to capture the knowledge of the lonely expert whose esoteric knowledge would die with him. Expertise in astrophysics, oil drilling in Alaska, and the like was what AI attempt to preserve. No doubt, there is an organizational equivalent of such esoterica—every company has all sorts of arcane knowledge.

However, the rare skills should *not* be the focus of learning. The most good occurs by taking an organization's most common jobs and creating training for them, not the top positions or the few that are critical. Organizations can gain the competitive edge by improving the jobs performed by lots of people. There's such volatility in organizations today that the cost of re-training new people becomes prohibitive. It's far less expensive to hand a new hire a computer disk than it is to put him or her through a classroom-based course.

The other compelling reason to train the many is the fact that more firms are becoming global corporations. An organization's most common jobs can exist in the United States, Japan, France, and Kenya. Although some differences exist in how one job is performed in various parts of the world, global organizations want uniform philosophies, policies, skills, and products. If the objective is to achieve this uniformity, standardized learning using tools such as simulations are needed.

PUTTING THESE RULES TO WORK FOR TRAINING

Trainers probably have read other books that contained great ideas that worked in theory but not in practice. Perhaps the HR and training staff have been burned by some other professor who came up with an ingenious work model that was impossible to implement.

Virtual learning isn't theoretical speculation. The ideas in this book have been successfully applied across a wide range of organizations. Although the clients don't have 20 years of data about their results as yet, they do have a great deal of empirical evidence. Teams from ILS and LSC have helped companies design and launch computer simulations that focus on many types of skills. Teams have designed and launched role-playing scenarios that help people acquire equally diverse skills.

The next five chapters will communicate how these simulations and scenarios incorporate the learning principles discussed here and how the resulting training is far more effective than in the past. The companies discussed will be Andersen Consulting, Diamond Technologies, Anixter Corp., Target, and Bennigans. The chapters don't describe dry case histories that merely describe what happened. What's important is the thinking that went into designing the simulations and scenarios, the obstacles that had to be overcome and the reactions of everyone from top executives to trainees to results of virtual learning.

5 CHAPTER

Andersen Consulting:

The Perfect Laboratory

Andersen Consulting was the first company to implement virtual learning. That firm presented an opportunity to transform the learning system of an entire organization. And not just any organization—the world's largest consulting firm, responsible for developing 40,000 people annually in offices worldwide. Even better, Andersen maintains a state-of-the-art training facility in St. Charles, Illinois, and the capabilities (from a software development standpoint and otherwise) to create all sorts of goal-based scenarios using computer simulations and role-playing. Best of all, Andersen's managers were open and eager to try anything that was effective—they weren't scared off by concepts like virtual learning, failure, or the idea of making learning fun.

When the team started to design the simulation, I felt like a kid in a candy store. Though to any Andersen executive who was skeptical about their huge investment, a more apt analogy might be Dr. Frankenstein in the laboratory.

HOW AND WHY THE EXPERIMENT BEGAN

This case history is pertinent because it gives you a sense of the possibilities virtual learning offers. Sometimes people think that goal-based scenarios are only viable in limited ways; that they only are effective given certain circumstances for certain types of people. At Andersen, we had the chance to help lots of different people learn lots of different skills. Few organizations required its people to learn such a diverse group of topics.

Andersen has always been a leader in training. Its managers believed that consulting skills aren't taught (or at least, taught well) in university environments or even in business schools, so the firm had better take on that responsibility and do a good job of it. Even before building their St. Charles training facility in 1970, the firm had placed a much greater emphasis on educating its employees than its competitors did.

Though the partners certainly were satisfied with their training, Andersen's top management was concerned by two issues that were brewing in the '80s. First, managers recognized that training employees was becoming much more complex than in the past. New technologies, rapid growth, and other issues demanded deeper and broader consulting skills, and these skills were not simple to teach or easy to learn.

Second, the Chicago area was not exactly a hotbed of computer science. With its headquarters in Chicago and its close ties with area universities such as Northwestern, Andersen wanted to help the area become competitive with both coasts.

For these reasons, Andersen brought me from Yale University to Chicago and helped establish the Institute for the Learning Sciences at Northwestern University. Although ILS required an enormous financial investment, it was nothing compared to Andersen's investment in revamping training for its business professionals. What the firm asked me to help the trainers do was convert a significant percentage of training materials from classroom/manual instruction to goal-based scenarios.

There was a third reason for doing all this: Cost reduction. Andersen invests more than $200 million per year in training its people. Much of that investment has to do with bringing professionals from around the world to the St. Charles facility, housing and feeding them. If a percentage of that training could be turned into "multimedia distributed teaching" (or, more colloquially, software), the partners would save millions of dollars. If the time it took to train people in certain skills was reduced by using goal-based scenarios, the firm would save millions more.

All this came to pass, and certainly Andersen's managers were pleased at the cost and time savings. In the process, they discovered that not only were their people learning faster for less money, but they were learning better. More than anything else, the power of virtual learning inspired Andersen to expand the program so that now 26,000 of the staff learn through goal-based scenarios annually. Much of the credit for this has to go to John Smith, head of Andersen's training facility, and his people who have embraced these new learning techniques and integrated them into their systems. Before you hear about the first major learning program they implemented, you should understand their training context.

SKILLS VERSUS KNOWLEDGE

As you can see from the matrix that follows, Andersen divides learning into skills, knowledge, individual process, and group process. The firm uses goal-based simulations depending on where in the matrix a particular learning objective falls. All knowledge learning is done in traditional ways. If the need is for people to learn *about* something, trainers won't use goal-based scenarios. When the need has to do with skills—with learning how to *do* something—trainers will employ simulations. If the learning goal is an individual process and skills, it will probably translate into goal-based scenarios on a computer. If it's a group process and skills, it may involve goal-based scenarios in a role-playing situation.

This matrix gives Andersen an analytical tool to determine when a simulation is warranted. Creating such clear delineations has helped the firm reengineer from classroom to goal-based learning, from "page-turning" computer-based training to computer simulations.

The transformation has also changed Andersen's philosophy about what training can accomplish. In the past, the training was

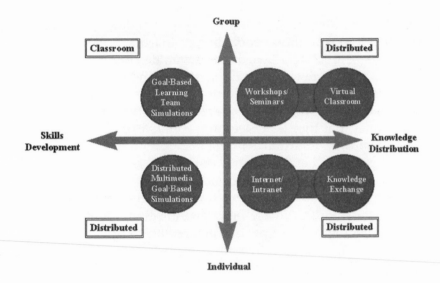

used to get professionals "ready to learn"; they'd do their actual learning in client engagements. Now they've shifted toward having that first learning-by-doing experience take place in a training environment rather than on the job at the client's expense.

This all sounds so simple and logical now. At the time, however, Andersen was demonstrating something many companies lack: a vision of what training can be. Rather than looking at it as a necessary evil, the managers were seeing training as adding value. The notion of shifting some of professionals' skill acquisition from the field to the "classroom" was revolutionary.

TEACHING PEOPLE THE BUSINESS

About two-thirds of Andersen's consultants lack business degrees; many of these people have technology backgrounds. As a result, trainees desperately need to acquire basic business skills such as cashflow planning and market analysis. For years, Andersen put these people through a Business Practices School (BPS) that involved about 80 hours of work—40 hours of workbook exercises in their home offices and 40 hours of classroom lectures at the St. Charles facility. Most of the material consisted of decomposing the content of slides and was as boring as studying a flowchart diagram sounds. It was Business 101, a survey course that emphasized memorization and (with the exception of some instructive stories told by good teachers) deemphasized experience.

The ILS team took the lessons Andersen hoped the course would teach and turned them into a computer simulation called BPC—Business Practices Course. One part of the simulation, for example, is about human resources. During the simulation the user becomes the HR person for Perrin Printing and Publishing, with responsibilities including hiring and firing, pay increases, counseling, and other managerial tasks. The simulation "lasts" 48 months, and during that time the user is faced with a mind-boggling array of issues, decisions, and consequences:

- Users have to decide who to send to a training program, and if they make the wrong decision, they cause morale problems.
- Users have an employee who's a nice guy but can't seem to become productive even though users try a number of approaches. The users fire him and are faced with a wrongful discharge suit.
- A department supervisor suddenly retires and users don't have anyone ready to take her place.

The simulation keeps throwing situations at trainees, asking them to make decisions as month after month goes by. The consequences of those decisions are played out on the computer screen, and all sorts of real-life consequences happen—users get reprimanded, commended, or fired. As the scenario unfolds, people appear on the screen in videotaped form to tell users stories related to the decisions they're facing or their consequences.

Everyone fails. But it's a fun, private failure that encourages learning. People who have taken this course routinely compare computer-simulated war stories about how they got fired or what they messed up in BPC. To listen to them, you might think they were describing events that really occurred. Perhaps that's the proof that a simulation was effective and learning took place—participants talk about it as if it were real.

WHEN LEARNING GETS COMPLICATED

Every organization has a wide spectrum of skills it needs its people to learn. Some are relatively straightforward, like the business practices just discussed. Others, however, are more complex and time-sensitive. Companies need their people to learn sophisticated skills and learn them fast in order to maintain a competitive edge.

The next chapter explores Andersen's Requirements Analysis simulation, recreating the experience using "screens" from the actual program. For now, here is an overview of what it entails and how it evolved.

Information engineering has become a key trend in the technology world. When Andersen's consultants are called on to do systems work, information engineering skills are essential. The ability to translate user requirements into technology requirements for programmers is prized. If consultants lack this skill, expensive rework results. A requirement is missed or misinterpreted early on in the process and rears its ugly head much later. In most instances, Andersen people have to go back in and fix things at the firm's expense—millions of dollars in writeoffs occur for want of information engineering skills.

Andersen, of course, had attempted to get its people who possessed those skills to teach others. Trainers would bring the experts to St. Charles to teach classrooms filled with younger, less experienced consultants. This approach didn't work for two reasons:

- **It was still teaching by telling**. The technologically complex subject went in one ear and out the other of most people who sat listening to the lectures.
- **It was impractical**. The information engineering experts were the ones Andersen could least afford to have in the classroom. These consultants were in great demand by clients, and to have them rotating in and out of the St. Charles facility was not good business.

For these reasons, the LSC team created a requirement analysis simulation that helped people learn this skill from data, event, and activity models. The three-module program began with an assignment to model the requirements of a restaurant for a client from another planet that had absolutely no experience with the concept of restaurants. (The next chapter will introduce you to client Zed from outer space.)

COACHING

The designers could only build so much software or so many role-playing GBSs for Andersen. Eventually the trainers had to learn to do it themselves (while our team remained in the background, providing guidance). One of their first efforts on their own had to do with coaching.

Most organizations will tell you that soft skills are hard to teach. At a time when soft skills such as teamwork, leadership, and the like are increasingly valued, companies are discovering how difficult it is to impart those skills to employees. Andersen had the same problem with helping its people acquire coaching skills. Part of the problem was that everyone believed he or she already was a good coach. Andersen surveyed different levels of managers, and they all responded exactly the same way when asked about their coaching ability: "I'm a good coach, but my supervisor isn't."

If you recall one of virtual learning's oft-stated learning rules, you'll understand why this response posed a problem: *The learner needs to be motivated to learn.*

Most of Andersen's people felt that they were doing fine and dandy in the coaching area; how could Andersen provide them a goal that would motivate them; why would they be interested in acquiring a skill they felt they already possessed?

Although most of Andersen's staff liked to think they were good at coaching, they didn't have a bedrock certainty about how good they were. They had never been forced to analyze this ability. There were no coaching tests, no pressure to perform in this area. It was easy and comforting to assume that one is a good coach. They needed to make their employees question that assumption. To do so, Andersen planned sessions at the St.

Charles facility where employees would be called on to coach a team of nine. They would simulate a client engagement in which they took on the role of coach, and they would be judged by their peers in terms of how proficient they were at this role.

Before this role-playing began on Monday, the course designers asked these "coaches" whether they wanted to go through some training and brush up on their coaching skills on the weekend prior to Monday's session. Not wishing to embarrass themselves in front of their peers, virtually everyone enthusiastically agreed that some learning in this area was in order. Thus, motivation.

The actual computer simulation the trainers built involves two modules, the first of which is about 3.5 hours long. It consists of a series of vignettes related to coaching—participants watch people do everything from coach masterfully to fail miserably at this task. After watching the vignettes, each person has to make a presentation to five other people in the program about what coaching should be. Trainees are allowed to illustrate their presentations with portions of vignettes, using the mouse to "excerpt" scenes that illustrate topics such as when someone missed a good opportunity to coach or made an astute intervention. After the presentation, they listen to others in the group share their ideas about coaching.

All of this is highly involving—people presenting their ideas about this personal skill are forced to confront parts of themselves that they might not be fond of (and that might prevent them from doing a good job of coaching). The emotional involvement is vital to learning, imprinting the experience in one's memory.

ILS's team taught Andersen to use the team's Guided Social Simulation (GuSS) tool, which enabled trainers to create a computerized scenario in which trainees attempt to coach others. This is sophisticated stuff; the simulation can't be put together in the same way as one for a more definable skill like operating a cash register. Coaching involves more variables—a novice can define the right and wrong ways to operate a cash register better than the right and wrong ways to coach. As a result, Andersen needed to create coaching scenarios that were not only true to their experiences but that allowed trainees to fail and respond to that failure in a variety of ways.

This computer simulation works hand in hand with the role-playing process that begins on Monday. The just-in-time learning is immediately applicable in a "live" setting, and participants get a chance to practice what they've learned. All of these activities reinforce the lessons and increases the odds that they'll stick with people and be usable later on.

WHEN TRAINEES HAVE TO LEARN IT LIVE

Andersen trainers have certain skills they want to impart that don't require computer simulations. Some skills are better learned through interactions with actual human beings rather than simulated ones. Trainers were able to create script role-playing scenarios that functioned as effectively as the computerized ones. Although it might seem easier to create a role-playing scenario than one using software, that's not always so. Although with live action designers don't have the technology issue or its associated expense to deal with, they do have to create verisimilitude. Learning isn't going to take place if participants find the scenario unbelievable, ludicrous, simple-minded, or otherwise unrealistic. All the learning rules of computer simulations still apply: *People need to be motivated to learn, they have to experience expectation failure, the learning process should be fun, and the learning should be story-based.*

Developing Integrated Solutions by Specialists

Andersen's scenarios incorporate all of these traits. One of the most successful live-action sequences is called Architecting Business Change, designed for young executives who need to learn behaviors necessary for working well in groups and with senior executives. The impetus for this scenario was the recognition that an increasing number of clients were hiring Andersen wanting "integrated" solutions. Instead of just wanting a technology solution or some other specialized answer, clients wanted broader concepts and holistic thinking.

The problem Andersen faced was that its people are specialists. Because of the growing complexity of every field, the consultants specialize out of necessity—they need to know more about their given field than their predecessors ever did. At the same time, when consultants go out on client engagements, they must be able to integrate ideas and knowledge from other specialties. To do so, the consultants require communication, teambuilding, listening, and relationship skills. If the young consultants acquire these skills, they work better in cross-functional teams and with senior executives.

The Tiger Electronics Scenario

With all this in mind, Andersen's trainers created a scenario entered into by five teams of six members each. They came to St. Charles and were directed to a conference room where they were greeted by their "client," the CEO of Tiger Electronics. This distinguished, gray-haired gentleman playing the CEO had also lived the role—he'd been a CEO of a major company before retiring. He introduced himself to the team as follows:

> Tiger is in the middle of a fight for its life. If we don't get the next five or six years right, we might as well write off our entire investment. We've had some consultants helping us with strategy, and we're satisfied with what they've done. But those consultants don't have the reputation for making things happen, and you guys do. However, you also have the reputation for making things happen in spite of the client; of making things happen over your clients' dead bodies. I'm telling you we hear things about you that indicates we might not be able to have a comfortable working relationship. What I'm asking you to do is this: Pick several key people and spend a week with us. I've taken my four key executives off their line

responsibilities, and they and I are available to you 24
hours a day. We'd like to meet with you tomorrow and hear
your reactions to our strategy, tell us whether you think
we've got them right. We need that common ground. Then
on Friday, we'll meet and talk about the type of action plan
we should put together to implement that strategy, the
proper sequence, and any crucial elements missing from
our strategy. We know you can't do all this in great detail
in a week, but we don't know if we want to invest two or
three months of staff time required for this if we don't like
your working style. . . .

The next 24 hours are chaos. In the words of Andersen's
John Smith, "They spend the first day describing the elephant
from their point of view." Everyone is talking and no one is listening. They become frustrated, go off down the wrong road,
and fail in ways too numerous to mention. All of this is great.
Remember, the goal is to help these people learn to work across
their various competencies and come up with integrated concepts for clients. They need to realize how bad they are at working in this manner and feel the wrath of the client before they can
become more effective integrators. Typically, the CEO in these
sessions will reprimand the team or the facilitators observing
these sessions will intervene when the team can't get untracked.

In one instance, a team asked a facilitator to comment on
their communication skills, and the facilitator said, "Picture six
television sets turned on and facing each other; you're broad-
casting, but you're not listening. You're so intent on convincing
everyone in the group that your model is the right model that
you haven't heard a thing the other people have said."

As the week goes on the team, guided by the comments of
senior executives and facilitators, learns from its failures.
Andersen's trainers could lecture until they're blue in the face
about the need to work cross-functionally and how people can
do so. But when trainers put people in a situation where their
specialization-induced myopia causes them to screw up, they'll
learn the skills necessary to work across boundaries.

OVERCOMING THE TWO MOST COMMON OBSTACLES

The ILS team had to overcome a variety of obstacles to implement virtual learning at Andersen. Those obstacles included the usual suspects—time and money—but also involved two issues that always arise when implementing this type of learning system.

The first one is *story-gathering*. Stories are the raw material of goal-based scenarios. Some are used in edited, videotaped form in computer simulations; others spawn the situations in which trainers place people. When interviewers ask experts for stories about their expertise, a lot of these veterans pontificate for the camera—they deliver their stories as lectures. What the designer wants is for people to personalize and dramatize their experiences—to make them immediate and memorable.

Sometimes the people with the best stories are the worst storytellers. They talk in monotones or are overly stiff, nervous, or affected. It is important to get experienced interviewers to do the interviewing, but sometimes even that doesn't help. Television reporters tend to interview in a manner that is not story-oriented; newspeople either want sound bytes or they let people go on and tell multiple stories at length. Obtaining experts' stories that are short and to the point takes practice.

The second obstacle has to do with *measurement*. Determining the effectiveness of this type of learning process is a bugaboo for organizations hung up on grading systems. Andersen recognized the difficulty of measuring its new training using traditional measurement tools. Still, managers needed to demonstrate to management that the process was working. The empirical evidence was overwhelming—the training folks documented that people picked up skills they lacked faster and more effectively than similar trainees using the old training methods. Feedback from program participants confirmed that they too felt this was the case. More important, perhaps, was the follow-up evaluation conducted by the training group. They asked supervisors of trainees whether their expectations were met, whether their people acquired the desired skills, and many other questions. Again, the response was overwhelmingly positive.

All of this is important for any organization to consider before implementing goal-based scenarios. Andersen is a good model for companies to benchmark before moving forward with a new learning process. The best argument for Andersen's innovations, however, comes via a detailed examination of one of its simulations. The next chapter will demonstrate how aliens, restaurants, and other unusual tools can make virtual learning an enormously effective process.

6

CHAPTER

ANDERSEN CONSULTING'S COMPUTER SIMULATION:

A System Explored from the Inside Out

Every organization has some skill set that's critical to its success yet that's difficult to impart. Try as the trainers might, the company can't train their people properly and the bottom line is threatened—customers or clients complain. Usually the skills are complex and the experts who possess the desired skills are scarce.

What does the trainer do? What Andersen Consulting did was to work with the ILS team to create a computer simulation that teaches new consultants requirements analysis.

Let's pause for a moment and acknowledge that requirements analysis doesn't sound like exciting stuff. If you're not with an organization in desperate need of this particular skill, you may be tempted to skip this chapter. If you do, it will just be that much more difficult to teach a critical, complex skill to people in your organization. You'll end up doing what trainers and teachers usually do when they're desperate to have someone learn it: attempt to pound the knowledge into learners' heads, fact by painful fact. Educators force learners to memorize how to do something, test them on how well they remember to do it, give rewards to people who score the best on the tests and implore them to learn this skill well while hoping to convince learners how important it is to learn it.

STIRRING UP LEARNERS' DESIRE TO LEARN

This chapter offers you an alternative. Every company has its version of requirements analysis. Part of the challenge is to find a way to make people interested in learning the skill. As the team from ILS began working on this project, the members knew we had to avoid boring or overwhelming trainees; the goal was to make the learning fun and accessible. Rule 8 from Chapter 4 advised trainers that "training should open with a bang." Leaders should get trainees involved quickly by having them do something interesting rather than numbing their minds with introductory telling. The team's vehicle for doing this was unorthodox; some people at Andersen no doubt felt it was a bit off-the-wall. But as strange as this concept might seem at first, it was a logical choice from a learning perspective.

It's to Andersen's credit that the partners trusted the simulation designers' judgment. The firm had a lot riding on this computer simulation. Information engineering had become a hot practice area, and Andersen needed to raise their people's proficiency in it to maintain their competitive edge. On a number of Andersen's client engagements, requirements analysis mistakes were made early that didn't surface until much later in the process—the resulting rework cost Andersen a great deal in dollars and client relationships.

The managers were counting on having their people make the mistakes and experience the rework during the simulation, thus avoiding repetition of these costly problems in the field.

AN ALIEN CONCEPT

Hi, I'm Zed. I need your help. I want to be ready for humans when they come. The right food. The right seating. The right gravity. How on earth the waitress system works. I figure when on earth, do as earthlings do: Hire a consultant. I need a set of rules that waitresses can use to do their jobs correctly. . . .

To paraphrase Dorothy, we're not in training's Kansas anymore.

This is the first of three modules in the requirements analysis course. In it, Zed requests help in setting up a restaurant in his own galaxy. The problem is that for Zed, restaurants are an alien concept. He needs someone to document the user requirements. To do so, consultants are shown a video clip of a typical restaurant scene—a man comes in, sits down at the table, looks at the menu, orders, and receives his food. The entire process is captured in the video clip, as well as elements that are extraneous to the process—the man is reading a newspaper, the waitress talks with someone else about a car accident, and so on.

From viewing this, trainees document user requirements for Zed. The consultants are asked to designate objects, events, and activities that are important to the process. After doing so, their input is used to create Zed's restaurant, and Zed sends a video clip featuring scenes of the restaurant in action. Because of the inevitable mistakes people make, they receive a clip like the following:

A couple enters the restaurant, but they sit there for a long time without a waitress approaching them. The man says, "She's been to every table but ours. Why is it so hard to get a waitress to take our order?"

The waitress finally arrives and asks, "Are you folks ready to order now?"

"We could if we had a menu. Then we'd know what you serve."

The waitress gives him a blank look; it's clear she has no idea what a menu is.

Each mistake in documentation translates into a major problem at Zed's restaurant. As Zed says before showing the video clip, "I looked over your rules and there were a few things that aren't working well. Send me your changes as soon as you can."

Which, of course, is the next task for trainees. They fix their mistakes and rewrite their rules until Zed's Diner is functioning smoothly.

THE LEARNING PRINCIPLES BENEATH THE "VIDEO GAME"

Zed's video almost seems like too much fun to qualify as learning. If this is your reaction, blame our educational system, which inculcated the notion that fun and learning don't mix. Zed does have the interactivity and other bells and whistles associated with video games; it does pose a highly entertaining and challenging puzzle to solve. But it also incorporates many of the learning principles we've discussed earlier.

First, *it's immediately involving*, from both emotional and intellectual standpoints. There's no academic tone or dry lecturing to be found. Even the buzzwords are missing—requirements analysis isn't mentioned once. The barrage of jargon that traditionally accompanies these courses is missing. Also missing is the long-winded introduction about why participants are learning what they're learning. Zed grabs one's interest the moment he appears on the screen.

Second, *failure is inevitable*. Almost no one puts the rules down properly the first time. In fact, it takes many consultants five, six, or seven times to "get to Zed." Some people assume that they only have to create the "big" rules for Zed and the details will take care of themselves. Others forget a key rule or don't articulate it properly. Most believe that they've done it right the first time, however, and are met with expectation failure when they see what their rules produced (either via video clips or text for scenes that weren't easy to film). There are lots of ways to fail, but the failure is private and nonthreatening. The surprise of the failure and the challenge of the game encourage consultants to learn what they did wrong and how to correct it.

Third, Zed provides people with *motivation to learn*. Andersen's trainers could lecture its consultants about the relationship between requirements and rework; they could put up signs and issue memos about the importance of the relationship. But the lesson doesn't sink in until learners experience the impact of ignoring the relationship. If nothing else, Zed teaches that if trainees don't get the rules right at the beginning, they can expect memorably bad things to happen when the system is built. It's easy for consultants to translate this lesson to their own experiences on the job—the motivation for paying attention to the relationship suddenly becomes much more powerful.

It takes trainees about four hours to finish this first module. Then they move on to Module 2, which is as content-rich as the first module is content-free.

THE REAL, SIMULATED THING

I'm glad you're here, have a seat. I know you have a general understanding of requirements analysis, and that's just what we need. . . . Let me give you some background. . . . S&O is a company that's been having trouble with a computer system used on a software support phone line. Originally it supported a single line. Customers called a single 800 number. . . .

The system keeps track of customer name, ID number, and any problems the customer may have. But lately, S&O support specialists have been overloaded with requests from customers for demo products about S&O software applications. They want to know when the next software application is coming out, for instance. We want to be responsive to customers, satisfy customers' needs for information, and build a reputation for being client-focused. We want customers to come back to the company so it can sell them more products. But support people just can't handle all the calls. That's why they've brought us in to analyze, understand, and model the requirements for an upgrade.

So begins the video clip for the second module. Consultants find themselves in a simulated client engagement where 90 percent of the work has already been completed. The remaining 10 percent, however, is problem-filled, and the consultants are expected to fix those problems through requirements analysis. The phone company client's 17 problems range from the relatively easy to the relatively complex, and consultants are given two days to solve them.

It can be tough going at first, which is exactly how the ILS team designed it. The amount of detail and the difficulty of the problems conspire to drive consultants a bit nuts—kind of like a real client engagement. Invariably, learners make a wrong decision as they're putting the requirements together. In some instances, the mistake is serious enough to crash the new phone system. Imagine what would happen if a company's phone system actually did crash because a consultant failed to do the requirements work properly. There would be hell to pay, and the scenario attempts to dramatize this hell when the system crashes before the consultant's eyes and the client becomes furious.

This type of failure grabs people's attention; they don't easily forget what they did that caused such chaos, even if it's simulated chaos.

At these failure points, trainees are eager to learn; they're also willing to ask for assistance. Because people learn in different ways, the module provides options for getting through the program, as the following screen demonstrates:

If people fail or get stuck, they can choose from a number of tools: a coach (who knows what learners have done, haven't done, and are supposed to do); a "gadget" for doing requirements analysis; a requirements analysis model; a reference system; and so on.

Even though most people won't use all these options, it's important to have them there. People have different learning styles. Some consultants rely on the coach to help them. Others like to use the reference tools and figure things out independently. The key is that the program is flexible; it lets people fail and correct mistakes according to personal preference.

It also connects memories. People learn when one experience summons another, similar one from the past. An old girlfriend left a guy five years ago because he was a macho pig; a new girlfriend left this guy today for the same reason. What he didn't learn the first time he might learn now. The cumulative force of these experiences causes him to sit, take notice, and respond with different behaviors.

Here, the second module recalls experiences from the first one. For instance, at one point the coach explains data models this way:

> Data models represent your clients' essential business data as well as the policies and rules that are necessary for their business operation. Now if you think about your engagement at Zed's Diner, there were several instances of essential business data that the system needed to track and manipulate like the menu, food and drink orders, these were essential objects to Zed's business and the system. The data model translates these objects into entity types. . . .

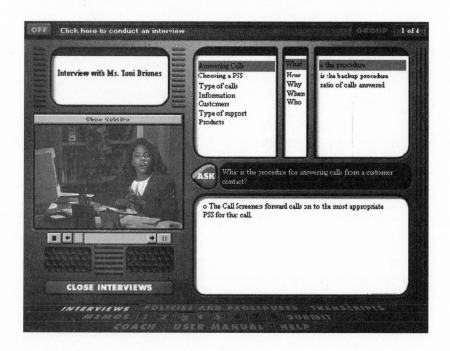

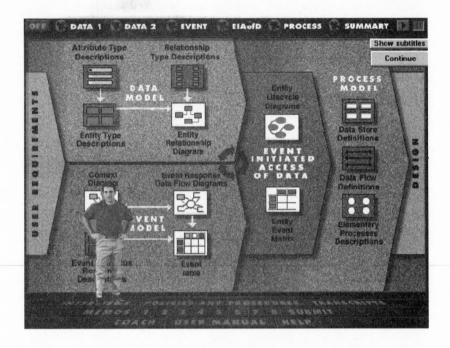

The simulation is also filled with war stories. Before creating this program, ILS's team surveyed Andersen's people to determine what the most common novice errors relative to requirements analysis were; team members also requested stories that illustrated why and how these errors happened. Invariably (and by computer design), consultants make these same errors when learners work on the S&O client engagement, and these stories are told when the errors are made.

STARTING FROM SCRATCH

Before getting into the third module, I want to relate a common experience I have with people I work with—students, employees and clients. They'll present something they've done, I'll tell them, "It's not right, do it again," and they begin peppering me with requests for guidance:

- What's wrong with it?
- What should we do to make it right?
- Can you pinpoint where we should start?
- Is there one section we should focus on?

Recall another rule from Chapter 4: "People are their own best teachers." If I tell these co-workers what to do, no learning will take place. If I give them lots of ideas, they won't discover any on their own. So I place them in the midst of the situation, like one of those survival courses; you drop trainees in the woods without anything except some matches and the skills they've been taught and let them learn how to survive. Those are essentially the feelings engendered among trainees using Module 3.

No work has been done on the requirements analysis assignment when consultants arrive in this last module. They really are on their own here as they document system requirements for an investment house client. Unlike the one-on-one approach of the previous two modules, consultants work on the assignment in teams (they sit together in front of the computer). Unlike the previous two modules, the support system isn't as strong. Because they can draw on learning from the first two programs, consultants are expected to be more self-reliant. Though the coach still exists, he or she is more impatient and less willing to dispense advice. For instance, if a learner asks the coach for help at what is deemed "inappropriate" moments, the coach will appear and tell the participant in a stern voice: "Why are you coming to me now? These models aren't nearly completed. You're going to have to go back to the user requirements and do more work. Come back when the models start reflecting the client's business."

Module 3 places the learner the closest to reality. Failure in this module can mean the crash of the investment company's system that tracks stocks, an obviously cataclysmic event that earns the consultants a tongue-lashing from the client. Though an expert's stories are used to help people deal with these failures, consultants are expected to work out problems on their own. As emphasized earlier, emotion is a factor in learning, and responses to this module can get emotional. Dramatic events take place, and the video clips include various people reacting emotionally to these events. Let's look at one example:

Hi, I'm Ellen. I'm the manager of this engagement.
. . . I understand you have some back-end client analysis;
that's good, your experience will help us out. Let me tell
you what we're trying to do at Continental Equity. The
managers called us in to model a mutual fund management system. When we were just starting our user requirement work, one of the first people we met was
Laura, a mutual fund manager at Continental. She was
calculating mutual fund asset value by hand! Because of
this manual process, many times it was incorrect.

The video clip switches from Ellen to Laura, who
appears frazzled as she says,

Please not now, I'm busy. Oh, it's you. I know it's
4:30. I'm almost done, but I just don't have net asset
value totally calculated yet, let alone checked for accuracy. I realize that Mr. Walters is going to be unhappy.
All right, upset. Okay, he's going to be furious and he
has a right to be. You know how bad it looks to be late.
One thing we *don't* need is another scandalous review
in a business magazine. But doing this by hand takes
more time than I'm given. . . .

As consultants work their way through the simulation,
they are likely to make the same mistakes that people in the field
most commonly make. For instance, one of the most frequently
cited errors was missing a key event that's not transparent to the
system but one the system needs to respond to. Put more simply,
this mistake results from overlooking critical data that's essential for a system to function effectively. In Module 3, most consultants fail to recognize that they had to go "outside" to the
New York Stock Exchange and get a feed for a mutual fund rate.

As one consultant wrote in describing his most memorable
learning experience from the simulation: "It never dawned on
me that all the data the client wants wouldn't be there. It never
dawned on me that the system would need something that
wasn't inside the company."

LOGICAL QUESTIONS

Reading all this, you probably have more questions than I can answer about Andersen's experiences with this computer simulation. Although I can't anticipate every question, I have anticipated some and have tried here to provide the answers.

Aren't Andersen's More Cynical Consultants Resistant to Learning from a Simulation Using a Creature from Another Planet?

Of course. Andersen's consultants are smart and sophisticated. Like many sharp business people, they are also skeptical of unproven (to them) methods and techniques. The Andersen culture encourages skepticism of concepts that seem pie-in-the-sky. When they first meet Zed, some consultants snicker and shake their heads in disbelief.

When they've completed the modules, however, just about everyone's resistance has melted. The simulation hits close to home—it causes the novices to fail at requirements documentation, a skill they realize they need to master. Their resistance to Zed and the other simulations melts as they fail and then find a way to solve a problem that caused their failure.

Don't People Get Frustrated Working on Seemingly Tough Problems?

The system is designed so that frustration levels don't reach a critical mass. People naturally get frustrated when they fail repeatedly, and some consultants take longer than others in moving through the program. But the edge is taken off the frustration in a number of ways. The first module is so much fun, it's hard to feel dejected or defeated—it's just a game, after all. The second module provides people with a wide range of resources when they fail—they're never left alone and resource-less with their failures. By the third module, most consultants have developed enough skill at requirements analysis that they can rebound from failure by trying a new idea on their own. In addition, the modules are all designed so that some problems can be solved easier than others.

When people use what they've learned to deal effectively with a situation, they're much more willing to tackle a more challenging problem. Most consultants are able to make some progress toward their goal in between failures, and that lessens their frustration.

How Does This Simulation Accommodate the Different Skill Levels and Learning Styles in Groups of Consultants?

Individualization is relatively easily, actually. The program designers recognized that some consultants will solve problems easier than others. The system is designed to enable people already possessing the skill to move quickly through until they come to a problem that challenges them. The designers also recognized that some people like to learn from humorous situations, others from examples, still others from fact-finding, and so on. There are multiple paths through the system, and it's up to each consultant to map his or her own path. How one learns from all this is self-controlled, a unique facet of this system and one critical to learning.

Is the Simulation the Perfect Learning Tool?

No tool is perfect. Each time Andersen trainers create one of these simulations, they've improved on the design of the previous one. Design failures exist in every simulation, and the designers have learned from their failures. In the requirements analysis modules, for example, the reference system is a bit boring and the interface (which enables users to access the menu) is somewhat complex. In Andersen's Business Practices Course described previously, there was no coach—a failure everyone obviously learned from in the requirements analysis course design. So this isn't a perfect learning tool; it's an imperfect learning tool that's a lot more effective than anything else that's available.

Can Simulations Be Designed to Help People Learn Any Skill They Need?

Theoretically simulations can teach anything, perhaps. But Andersen teaches its people skills in a variety of ways. Trainers use scripted role-playing or "live" simulations to teach certain skills that are best learned through group interactions (the next chapter shows how the Diamond Technologies organization learns this way). Other skills aren't sufficiently important to spend all the time and money on creating a computer simulation. Others can be learned on the job. Andersen, like other clients I work with, tends to choose skills for computer simulations because:

- There's a general feeling that a skill is important and that people aren't particular proficient in that skill.
- There's a specific problem facing the organization, and they need specific skills to address it.

As of this writing, Andersen's next big computer simulation involves project management.

If People Have to Practice Failing to Make the Learning Stick, How Can People Practice a Simulation?

First, learners can practice mastering the simulation by going through it again. Second, learners naturally practice on the job—they'll fail in real life just as they did in the simulation. The difference is that they probably won't fail as fast or as badly because they've had the benefit of learning from their simulated failure. The learning process is accelerated, making practicing on the job less dangerous for the company and the client.

How Long Did Creation of the Three Modules Take?

Development of Andersen's simulation required 18 months of hard work. That may sound like a long wait for a company anxious to get its training up and running tomorrow, but it's really not that much longer than putting together an original, noncomputerized training program. Andersen's training designers have found that they're reducing the time frame as they become more proficient in designing these simulations—the Business Practices simulation took six months more than the Requirements Analysis one.

There just aren't many people who know how to design computer simulations, so it's not just a problem of figuring out how to teach employees a critical skill. Trainers also face the challenge of acquiring the design skills necessary to teach that skill.

What If a Smaller Company Can't Afford to Build a Simulation?

Read the next chapter.

7

CHAPTER

Diamond Technology:

A Precious Role-Playing Lesson

What if you're not in a large company like Andersen? What if the company can't afford to create a computer simulation (or doesn't have the budget at the moment)? What if the firm is smaller in size or at least smaller in its training capabilities?

Such companies can take advantage of virtual learning without computers through goal-based scenarios.

Diamond Technology Partners is a consulting firm that implemented noncomputer goal-based scenarios with great results. Though I hesitate to use another consulting firm as an example, Diamond offers an irresistible story to tell: how a small, fast-growing company helps a diverse group of people learn difficult new skills quickly.

EVOLUTION OF A ROLE-PLAYING SCENARIO

Diamond is a new strategy and technology consulting firm that hired 170 people in two years and continues to grow rapidly. As in any organization that experiences rapid growth, new people have to hit the ground running. As in any organization that's so young, it's tough to communicate and inculcate the desired corporate culture. As in any new consulting firm, the need is for people who are skilled at creating extraordinary means of looking at problems and producing solutions.

On top of all this, Diamond was hiring a diverse group of people from business schools, other consulting firms, and industry who all brought along different experiences and working styles. Certainly they were bright and talented people. But as Jim McGee, the partner in charge of the training effort, said, "Our biggest problem is that our people know how to do a lot of things, but they don't know *when* to do them." The new employees didn't know when to confront a client with an issue and when to let it slide; they didn't know when it was advisable to take a risk and when it made sense to play it safe. Communication and team skills were on Diamond's wish list, along with a desire to forge a common culture.

After about a year of being in business, Mel Bergstein, the head of Diamond, sent Jim McGee over to view our work at the Institute for the Learning Sciences. Jim, a former instructor at the Harvard Business School, found that ILS's approach dovetailed with the Harvard case study method—in his words, ILS was just "taking case studies to the next level." Jim recognized the benefit of creating goal-based scenarios and using failure as a catalyst for learning. Because Diamond was a relatively new company, it wasn't hamstrung by existing, outdated training practices and policies.

ILS's team began working with Diamond to "reverse engineer" its consultants' engagements in the field. The organization wanted to take apart the most common situations the consultants faced with clients and reconstruct these situations as a prototypical role-playing scenario. The managers' logic was sound: If they could create a scenario that looked and felt like a real field experience, people would recall it when they were on client engagements and similar scenarios unfolded. If the trainees screwed up during the scenario, they would remember it and be less likely to screw up in the field. And they'd learn fast. If properly crafted, a role-playing, goal-based scenario provides a prototypical experience, combining and distilling events that might take months to encounter in the field.

The role-playing approach made more sense than a computer-based one, not only for financial reasons but because Diamond wanted to help people learn to work together effectively in teams. The teams would be composed of different levels of employees from different backgrounds and skill sets, and it was critical for them to learn to function efficiently as a unit.

It figures that a company with the name of Diamond would start the process with something hard. As a pilot test, the managers decided to teach their people the one skill that everyone told them was too difficult to teach: Reengineering. When that worked exceptionally well, Diamond put together a second scenario that is described here.

A TYPICAL PRESSURE-PACKED CLIENT ENGAGEMENT

The reengineering scenario that our team built for Diamond called for a unit of consultants (from senior partners to junior associates) to analyze business processes and explore reengineering issues for a client. The second scenario takes place a year later. The client liked the team's earlier recommendations but decided to work on them without the consulting firm because "you're very expensive." Now, however, the client has deemed its internal progress too slow and invited Diamond's team back. Their mission is to analyze a series of projects and recommend the ones to keep, discard, and change.

The course lasts one week, and the teams are representative of teams in the field—they comprise a partner, a principal consultant, an associate consultant, and so on. In some instances, they have two teams working on the scenario simultaneously (but separately). At the end of the week, the course enables each team to see how the other dealt with the same issues.

There is a paradoxical quality to this type of learning. On the one hand, trainers want teams to take the scenario where they will—they need the freedom to make horrendous mistakes and rebound with ingenious ideas. On the other hand, trainers must exert some control or the role-playing can turn into chaos.

To strike the proper balance, our designers do the following:

- **Develop a detailed scenario**. Teams receive a written history of projects and other background that gives them a context in which to act. These scenarios provide boundaries that people have to observe—they are guided by what has taken place in the past.
- **Create the scenarios with failure in mind**. Diamond employees interviewed people in the field, asking them what mistakes were made in client engagements and what would they do differently. In creating the scenarios, the designers wanted learners to have every opportunity to make these common mistakes. In the first course Diamond offered, teams were told that their numbers must "tie together" when they present their financial analysis. Telling, of course, usually doesn't get the point across, as the following story illustrates. A consultant on one of the teams rose to make his presentation to the client's CEO, and it was clear that the numbers in the consultant's slides didn't tie together. The CEO slowly, politely, and memorably took apart the novice's financial logic for 10 minutes in front of all his team members. It was not an experience the presenter could easily forget.

   Another common mistake is building a "data warehouse" and neglecting to detail a way to extract data from old systems. Most people focus on the user interface and neglect this critical task. As a result, Diamond wanted to give teams every opportunity to make this exact mistake, and most of them do. Consultants expected to build a highly effective data warehouse because they did a good job with the interface; their expectations weren't met because they failed to figure out a way to extract existing data.
- **Motivate learners with a compelling goal**. Part of the controlling factor in scenarios is for team members to recognize the value of playing by the rules. In other words, most people take the scenario seriously because

they understand it will help them deal with problems they face in real client engagements. As the scenario unfolds, the team surmounts problems such as obstinate clients, difficulty in communicating ideas to team members, and obstacles in presenting viable recommendations to clients.

- **Use credible actors**. The people who play the leading roles in the scenarios—CEOs, CFOs, CIOs—occupied similar positions in the real world of work. Most of the ones Diamond hired, therefore, look and act the parts. They command respect and exert control over the process. Diamond correctly avoids using its own people to play these key roles; having a well-known associate play the CEO would bias people's reactions.

- **Monitor, provide feedback to, and tinker with scenarios**. Video cameras placed in the training rooms enable Diamond to monitor the sessions. In those rare instances when the team goes way off course, training supervisors intervene and get the team back on track. More typically, interventions are subtle and situational. For instance, trainers may be observing the team in action and come up with a great idea to present the group with a learning opportunity—at the next break, the trainers might suggest the client throw a curve at the consultants and see how they respond. Or trainers may talk to the team about why they're failing to confront a client about an important issue. At the end of the week, trainers debrief the teams and discuss their failures, examining why they failed and how they might have solved problems.

Despite these controls, teams are volatile and unpredictable. Even though Diamond has run these courses many times, the trainers are still surprised by what teams do. And that's great. The free-form nature of role-playing generates excitement and challenge. Knowing anything can happen makes learning fun.

THE ROLE THAT FAILURE PLAYS

The big difference between failure in a computer simulation and failure in role-playing is that the latter is more public. Diamond's trainers are smart about how to handle these public failures. When someone messes up during the scenarios, the trainee hears about it. The chastisement, however, is not the belittling, humiliating kind that stymies learning. Although it's not always gentle, the criticism focuses on the issue rather than the individual.

Encouraging failure is part of Diamond's culture. The organization's view of itself as a consulting firm is that its people come up with the solutions no other consulting firm can. This means the consultants have to take risks and fail at times. Role-playing demonstrates how failure is part of the Diamond culture; it also gets a lot of failure out of the way during use of the scenario rather than later on at the client's expense. Third, the role-playing demonstrates that nothing terrible happens when an employee fails and that something wonderful often occurs— learning. The following are a few examples.

Getting Fired by a Client

The team led by Anthony was having trouble with the client's CEO. Not only was there tension between the CEO and the team, but it seemed to them that the CEO was incompetent and preventing the organization from moving forward. At one of the meetings, a member of Anthony's team decided to see how hard he could push the CEO. Virtually calling the CEO incompetent, the team member said, "Ultimately, the shareholders will decide if we're right or you're right."

The CEO fired the team on the spot and threw them out of the room.

The team members didn't know what to do. It was midweek in the course; the scenario was predicated on working with the client. Only now the team no longer had a client; they didn't even have a room in which to meet. What were they supposed to do? The team members were befuddled; they couldn't believe what the CEO had done. Sure, they could have understood if he became angry. It wouldn't have surprised them if he had given them a warning. But getting fired was the last thing they expected, particularly in the middle of a week-long training simulation.

This is expectation failure at its finest. As trainers let the team stumble about in their confusion, team members learned something important about how to communicate with a client—or rather, how not to communicate. Even though this was a simulation, it had a real emotional and intellectual impact on the team. And in fact, the simulation spilled over into reality as everyone in Diamond quickly learned that Anthony's team had managed to get itself fired during the training course—word went out to Diamond people all over the world by fax, phone, and e-mail. People ribbed the members of the team mercilessly. In an odd way, the failure became celebrated (and still is to this day).

Of course, the learning didn't stop there. Diamond's supervisors gathered members of Anthony's team together and discussed the gestalt of client interaction. Sometimes instructors can give people the greatest advice in the world, but it won't penetrate because they're not in a mood to hear it. After this particular failure, Anthony's team was ready and willing to hear whatever expert advice trainers had to offer.

Delivering Bad News

Another common failure among teams is an inability to deliver bad news. In Diamond's second course, teams discover that their client's strategy is fatally flawed. Based on this discovery, the team has to inform the client that the organization can't implement the client's prized strategy and that the organization is in serious trouble. Most teams sugar-coat the bad news. They meet with the client and say euphemisms like, "Well, there's a little bit of a problem."

This is an instance in which trainers inform the team of their failure. Trainers clearly communicate that if the team were to sugar-coat this same bad news during a real client engagement, it could have terrible repercussions—bankruptcy of the client's firm being one of them. The training supervisors coach teams on how to deliver bad news and allow team members to practice it. Delivering bad news is a skill in which consultants need plenty of practice!

Sometimes a team member's failure is identified by another role-player in a single, dramatic moment. In one of Diamond's role-playing sessions, a trainee was giving a terrific presentation. He was eloquent, passionate, and completely convincing. When the presenter finished and sat down, he was beaming, obviously proud of himself. At that point, the lead partner on the team leaned over and whispered to him, "You forgot to ask for the work."

His change in complexion suggested that he had been bitten by a vampire. This particular consultant will never forget to ask for the work again.

CONTINUOUS IMPROVEMENT

Trainers, as well as trainees, benefit from their own failures during virtual learning sessions. One of the advantages role-playing has over computer simulations is that it's easier (and less expensive) to change. Diamond has made adjustments to both courses based on the trainers' and participants' observations and feedback. In some ways, what doesn't work the first time can produce what works best the next—they're the scenes in the scenario that have evolved from "second-generation" failure.

In the first course, for instance, teams were set loose on the reengineering problem and competed against each other. This was by design. Diamond had communicated that one team would win and one would lose. The intention was to fuel consultants' competitive fires. The result was that the two teams were at each other's throats. Intense competition was taking the fun out of the process (and perhaps taking much of the learning out of it). Diamond's managers recognized that they were sending the wrong message to the teams; they wanted trainees to learn to collaborate with one another, not fight like gladiators.

In one of the early courses, the competition was getting out of hand, so in the middle of the course, the supervisors called time-out and had both teams adjourn to a bar where they could socialize and swap stories. Observing the camaraderie that developed in the bar, the supervisors institutionalized the bar experience—teams in both courses now routinely take a Wednesday bar break. Though Diamond still runs two teams simultaneously, trainers have reduced the competitive tension considerably.

Another example of continuous improvement of the scenarios occurred recently as it became clear that teams weren't establishing solid relationships with chief information officers. In client engagements, Diamond had found that consultants failed to create good working alliances with CIOs. Designers thought the scenarios had been set up so participants would learn to take advantage of this potential alliance. Unfortunately, most of the consultants still ignored this opportunity, focusing on the CEO relationship. So in the middle of one role-playing scenario, trainers adjusted the script. During a meeting after a break, training leaders instructed the CEO to lose his temper during a meeting and ignore the agenda the team wanted him to follow. Trainers further instructed the CIO to calm the CEO down and get him back on track. Then trainers scheduled a separate meeting with just the CIO and the team to discuss what happened. The team seized the opportunity to forge a stronger relationship with the CIO, which in turn benefited them down the road.

The point of all this is: Don't set your role-playing scenario in stone.

BEYOND SKILLS

Diamond's objectives for the role-playing scenarios weren't just skill acquisition. As a young, fast-growing firm, the leaders wanted to build a tight-knit culture, and they saw an opportunity to do so through their training. Risk-taking, celebrating failure, creating unique solutions, client communication, and program management (to orchestrate change) were cultural principles Diamond wanted to imbue. But the managers didn't want to imbue the culture within the usual principles-to-practice order; a chronology in which the principles are taught through lecture and manuals and then put into practice. Diamond wanted people to learn these principles through practice. The role-playing was structured to enable this to happen.

It's worth noting what one young consultant said after going through the first course: "I thought what was important was the analytical basis of our work. But now I understand that it's also the rapport and relationship with the clients, how we communicate with them." There's no question that putting together a spreadsheet is a good skill for consultants to have. But Diamond wanted its people to learn the cultural imperative of client communication; the importance of being able to walk a reluctant client through a spreadsheet and buy into it.

An instructor can't teach that principle in a lecture. Or rather, the instructor can't expect someone to buy into it based on spoken words. Consultants who don't yet recognize the importance of client communication (and many of them don't) have to get a chance to fail at it and then practice what they've learned.

Diamond is justifiably proud of how its scenarios have helped people acquire new team, change management, and reengineering skills. But the trainers probably also would say that an equal or even larger accomplishment was forging the organization's desired culture.

IN THE PROCESS WE TRUST

For some people, virtual learning using role-playing requires a leap of faith. I mention this point for all of you who are considering implementation of role-playing scenarios. Computer simulations are easier to believe in for many companies and trainees. They're tangible products, the technology and product are impressive, and multimedia learning is hot.

Role-playing scenarios, however, can be effective for organizations like Diamond. To maximize their effectiveness, however, you can't be a control freak. If you think you can control what people learn, you'll be disappointed. Different people will learn different skills in different ways. Diamond's managers certainly wanted their consultants to learn process mapping from the course, but the leaders accepted the fact that not everyone would learn it; that some would only learn how important it was and have to pick up the skill at a later date, and that one person might learn one aspect of process mapping whereas someone else would learn another aspect.

At Diamond, certain scenario developers as well as consultant-trainees wanted to control what was learned. Some of the developers suggested supplementing the role-playing with lectures or written materials. Early in the course, some participants asked, "Where are the handouts?" and objected to the lack of traditional training.

Anyone attempting to implement role-playing scenarios should be prepared for these reactions. Almost all the participants who object to the process initially will be won over by the time it's done. They come to recognize the value of failure-based experience; it's so close to the real thing that trainees could legitimately put it on their resumes.

It's a bit tougher to get a buy-in from the training old guard. But hear the words of Diamond's training head Jim McGee: "Trust that if you provide the right context and a strong support base, your people will find something important to learn. If you get comfortable with the idea of letting people fail, they'll learn more than you imagined was possible.

8

CHAPTER

ANIXTER'S HIGHLY AMBITIOUS MODEL:

Moving to an Electronic Learning-on-Demand System

How does a fast-growing, global company selling 40,000 rapidly changing, high-tech products and services train its workforce of 5500 people?

That's actually one of the easier questions that leaders of Anixter Inc. asked themselves. More difficult ones included:

- How do we train novices not only in hard and soft skills, but in our organization's unique cultural values?
- Can we approach a "learning-on-demand" ideal that will help us reduce our dependence on expensive classroom-based training?
- It is possible to reduce our training costs if we have to make a significant investment in computers to help people learn electronically?
- Because we have so many new people and the skills we want them to master are relatively complex, can we reasonably expect any new learning system to be up and running effectively in the near future?

- Can we create an electronic learning curriculum that is modular; one in which we change pieces as our product lines and services change?

If these questions weren't enough to make a grown training designer cry, Anixter had established a strategic partnership with Lucent Technologies, and the two were moving together into markets throughout the world. Training people to work well with Lucent was a priority.

Although Anixter shared some of the same concerns as Andersen and Diamond, the former also was in a different position. Selling structured cabling products (products used to hook up computer, telephone, cable TV, and power systems) as well as services was one key difference. Perhaps more significantly, as a midsized organization Anixter lacked the enormous resources of an Andersen and the relatively small number of trainees of a Diamond. Like many companies, the firm required a training approach that balanced dollars and people. It had to be financially feasible, but it also had to be used by a lot of people.

To help you understand Anixter's thinking about training, you need a little history about what catalyzed the organization's interest in computer-based simulations.

PLANES, TRAINING, AND MOBILE PEOPLE

It's one thing to partner with another organization; it's something else for people to become skilled at making the partnership work. Anixter's partnership with Lucent Technologies in the early '90s required Anixter salespeople to understand what Lucent was all about, when Lucent should be brought into the client relationship, how Lucent should be used, and so on. Perhaps it sounds easier to do than it actually is. Partnering is a relatively new concept, and most people don't have much experience with how to partner. Anixter's new salespeople, for instance, didn't automatically put in a call to their Lucent counterparts when they should have, and they didn't think to request information from Lucent that might have helped them close a deal. Anixter's recently-hired salespeople needed to learn the intricacies of working with a partner.

Like Andersen, Anixter didn't want to pull top salespeople (or Lucent's) off the road and fly them in to teach in a classroom for weeks at a time when they could be making sales. It made much more sense to capture the reps' expertise and distribute it via computer. Lucent agreed with this idea and was willing to contribute funds to help create such a training tool.

Julie Anixter, head of the company's training division, began looking for someone to build computer-based training. She found a mind-boggling array of individuals and organizations who claimed expertise in designing multimedia-based systems. One company in particular impressed her. The quality of its systems was first-rate, at least visually—the sound and graphics were beautiful, and the systems seemed user-friendly. She hired the company to work on the Lucent-partnering training program, called Mastering Systimax Solutions.

Appearances Can Be Deceiving

It was a failure, and unlike a simulated failure, a somewhat costly one. After an investment of considerable time and money, Anixter realized that the designer had simplified what was inherently complex. The skills required to sell an Anixter/Lucent solution weren't as cut and dried as the computer training made them out to be. Anixter parted company with the designer after the first phase of the design work was complete and began looking elsewhere.

Anixter had learned an important lesson through its failure: *Don't judge a computer training program by its cover.*

As organizations jump on the multimedia-based training bandwagon, they are often like adolescents who begin dating; they're easily enticed by appearances. A lot of computer programs *look* like you can learn a lot from them. Smart training people who are computer neophytes are easily misled. It's the old "technology can conquer anything" syndrome: Build a system and trainees will come. If essential learning principles (goal-based scenarios,

failure, storytelling, and so on) aren't integral to the system design, it will be ineffective.

After Anixter's false start, the managers began searching
for a more effective designer of multimedia training. After coming across an article about the work of ILS and how it helped
Andersen, the managers contacted us and eventually contracted
to design Systimax.

The Revised Plan: Three Scenarios, Eleven Skills, One Culture

Companies like Anixter (as well as Anderson and Diamond) increasingly want two-for-one learning experiences; they want
their people to learn essential skills and at the same time absorb
the corporate culture.

To do this isn't as hard as it sounds. When you think about
it, the way many skills are used has a great deal to do with the
culture (a company that emphasizes ethical behavior will want
its people to learn how to make a sale without misleading the
customer, for instance). It's therefore important to design scenarios with both objectives in mind.

Let's start out by reviewing the skills Anixter wanted to
teach related to Systimax. The company wanted salespeople to
learn how to:

- Probe for customer needs.
- Develop a sales strategy.
- Consult on Systimax solution.
- Use resources effectively.
- Make a business presentation.
- Handle customer objections.
- Team with a supplier/partner (Lucent Technologies).
- Sell Anixter's value to gain a customer commitment.
- Sell higher in the organization.
- Research customers.

For many new salespeople, the Anixter culture was more foreign than any of the listed skills. Anixter is unlike many organizations in its extraordinary openness and informality. Titles don't really matter, the organizational hierarchy is almost as flat as a pancake, verbal communication is preferred over memos as a mode of communication, honesty is esteemed, service is deified. One look at the company's policy manual shows that this isn't IBM—the page on organizational structure is blank, and another section forbids people to call anyone Mr. or Ms.

To help people learn the culture and skills, the LSC team created the following three scenarios:

- A salesperson receives a lead about a software company that is moving into a new building. The trainee meets with the customer, identifies the prospect's needs, recommends a solution, and moves through the sales cycle until receiving a commitment.

- The salesperson has a contact at a large financial institution that has recently acquired a smaller bank. The trainee meets with the contact to verify the opportunity and attempts to sell Systimax as a corporate standard.

- Two systems integrators are recommended, and the trainee's goal is to get a commitment from both of them to bid Systimax and purchase materials from Anixter if awarded the job.

These scenarios all unfold on CD-ROM, and trainees "experience" them in a highly interactive manner. As trainees move through the scenarios, they field and make phone calls, attend meetings, give presentations, and use various resources. Woven throughout are videotaped clips featuring war stories and expert advice—trainees can access them at various appropriate points throughout the scenarios.

Now let's move from this rather dry description to a more visceral look at how Systimax functions.

SETTING TRAPS

You arrive at your office and are excited to find a new lead—
Chris Thompson at Horizon Software has been given your name
and wants you to call. Horizon is expanding its headquarters
building and needs structured cabling. Excited at what seems
like a great prospect, you pick up the phone and call Chris. You're
not prepared for Chris repeating Anixter's name questioningly,
saying he vaguely remembers someone calling him about
Anixter. You know you're about five seconds away from Chris
thanking you for calling and hanging up. What do you say?

Losing the Prospect

Most trainees struggle to keep Chris on the phone; most fail.
When Chris hangs up, a tutor appears on the screen and says,
"You have to gain Chris's interest in having a conversation. . . .
You have to figure out what he's doing and what he needs." The
tutor gives you options for learning how to do this. You can
choose to hear stories from 26 Systimax sales experts from
around the world; one of them sold the largest Systimax instal-
lation in history to Barclay's Bank in London. Or you take your
advice straight from the tutor.

However you take it, its arrival corresponds with your
point of failure. If the failure with Chris occurred on the job (and
as most salespeople know, such failures are common), you
would sit there staring malevolently at your phone. You would
be ready for advice, but none would be forthcoming—your boss
probably would be busy and the other person who might help
you would be on the road. By the time they'd be available, you'd
be past the point of learning; your failure would have been
pushed aside in favor of other issues.

The simulation, however, provides you with the expertise
you desire exactly when you want it. Even better, you can practice using that advice on Chris and see whether you can get this
amnesia-burdened prospect to listen. It might take a few failures
before you get Chris interested and secure a meeting, but the
timing and failures will imprint themselves on your mind.

The traps set in the system aren't artificial. The designers put them in place because Anixter's field research demonstrated that these were the ways its novice salespeople commonly failed. The trick became to set the traps naturally. Trainees shouldn't see them coming but rather should experience that stomach-knotting feeling when Chris only vaguely remembers the referral.

Forgetting Their Partners

One mistake many Anixter rookie salespeople make is forgetting to bring their Lucent counterparts into the sales process (or bringing them in too late in the process to do much good). In the computer simulation, there are no explicit instructions to get Lucent involved, and many trainees neglect this responsibility.

When this happens, Joan Van Kampen, an intimidating MIS manager at the prospective client's office, confronts the trainee and says, "Wait a second. If you guys have a strategic partnership with Lucent, how come no one from Lucent is here?" It's an embarrassing moment; trainees want to smack themselves on the forehead, as if to say, "How could I have forgotten something so basic?" The embarrassment increases the odds that they won't forget it again.

Incorporating the Corporate Culture

The cultural learning takes place on a number of levels. On the most basic level, Anixter experts who tell stories or give advice as part of the scenario communicate that culture. Their stories don't just focus on a specific skill, but on the way Anixter people use that skill. Cultural traits such as treating people with respect and being truthful and straightforward are spotlighted. At the same time, these people tell their stories in ways that are true to who they are. We worked hard to avoid using lectures or "presentations" of materials. From the CEO on down, Anixter's experts are informal, bright, funny, enthusiastic, and offbeat. They convey the qualities that are important to Anixter. On a more sophisticated level, the paths that take learners through the system are designed to encourage certain cultural traits. If learners try to play politics or do something underhanded in order to make the sale, they fail and then hear stories and advice related to why they failed.

AN INTEGRATED LEARNING SYSTEM

Anixter's managers did not want just one system to help people acquire one group of skills. The managers were far more ambitious than that, recognizing that they had an opportunity to transform the learning process within their organization. In fact, Anixter stipulated from the start that the systems be modular; trainers wanted to be able to replace certain elements with new ones to reflect changing organizational requirements (not a simple task from a multimedia perspective). Anixter wanted systems that were sufficiently flexible that they'd last for years.

As ambitious as the design of Systimax was, it was only one of five systems that LSC's team helped create. The other four comprise what Anixter refers to as its Foundation Learning Architecture, including:

- A selling system that uses simulations to help people handle a wide range of problems and opportunities in a sales environment.
- A corporate memory system designed to facilitate understanding of how things are done at Anixter; users can ask various questions about the company and get answers and stories from experts ranging from the CEO to inside salespeople.
- A coaching system that puts managers in scenarios designed to improve their coaching skills.
- A system that teaches salespeople to use automated selling software by simulating the top 10 most frequently used transactions.

One of the most challenging aspects of designing these systems—and something that makes them so effective—is that they accommodate the many paths along which people travel as they learn. If there were only one path through the system, only people who followed that path would learn anything. With this in mind, we designed scenarios that could be "solved" in many ways.

There's no single right way to do coaching, for instance. Anixter wisely didn't want systems that trained managers to coach in a prescribed way. Instead, the designers began trying to replicate the common ways Anixter people messed up when trying to coach. One of the reasons novices messed up was related to the coaching environment. Anixter's rapid growth resulted in many young managers being promoted and put in charge of established groups. This new boss/old staff situation made coaching a delicate process—the tension between new and old made a tough skill even tougher to master. Another tension point was between the inside and outside salesforce, as the following scenario demonstrates.

> One of your salespeople comes to you and complains that another salesperson isn't sharing leads. You have numerous options as to how you'll respond as a coach. You can tell the person what he should do, you can fix the problem yourself, you can read one or both of them the riot act, or you can have a dialogue with him and help him address the problem himself.

No matter what the trainee chooses to do, each path has perils. With the best of coaching intentions, the learner may try to help the salesperson work out his problems with the other fellow. The learner's efforts, however, can have the opposite effect and cause both salespeople to be at each other's throats. Or the learner's response may cause the salesperson to be upset with the learner/manager. Or the trainee may cause the other salesperson who's been accused of not sharing leads to storm into the office and say, "Let me tell you what's wrong with him (the guy who complained)."

Even if the trainee attempts to solve the problem through skillful listening, questioning, and paraphrasing, he or she may still fail. It takes practice to reach a resolution through coaching. Without such practice some managers might give up and revert to autocratic behavior.

Each trainee receives a great deal of practice at failing on his or her own particular path. Although coaching skills such as listening and questioning are constants, each person practices the skills in different ways.

ISSUES ALONG THE WAY TO CLASSROOM-FREE TRAINING

Anixter's training isn't there yet. Practice is essential for trainers as well as trainees, and Anixter is practicing how to use its five systems to learn from the failures that surface. Because one of the company's goals is for these systems to be modular, the trainers have to practice replacing pieces as new training requirements arise to ensure the systems continue to function effectively.

Before Anixter begins tearing out the blackboards from its classrooms and reselling the overhead projectors on the anachronistic training tools market, managers need to figure out the best way to deliver such systems to their people. It's an issue that faces every organization, and every organization has a slightly different plan and timetable for implementing the training. Anixter, for example, is creating awareness of these new systems and a buy-in for them by rolling them out through existing activities. The trainers placed the systems in kiosks in training centers and conference rooms, making them part of the natural corporate landscape. The systems now are part of orientation for new employees. The systems are being worked into the current training system. On top of all this, Anixter training people are *demonstrating* the systems all over the world. I stressed *demonstrating* because Anixter recognized the importance of showing rather than telling. As eloquent and inspiring as a speaker might be, he or she is no match for a demo of the system itself. Seeing how it works is much more effective than being told that it does. From the onset, the training group showed previously developed institute systems to Anixter's senior executives to obtain a buy-in.

Another interesting wrinkle to Anixter's buy-in strategy is that the Systimax program is part of a formal internal certification process. In the structured cabling industry, formal certification by an external industry group is important. Anixter has set up its own certification process (one reflecting the company's particular values), and the salespeople have to complete Systimax to be certified. This provides strong motivation to master the skills involved.

One issue that almost every organization faces when it does goal-based scenario training is: whether the modules provide a good return on the company's training investment. There was some initial resistance at Anixter to the cost of the technology (the high-powered computers) necessary to run the electronic learning systems. That resistance was lessened somewhat by the knowledge that the systems would get key people off airplanes and out of classrooms, giving them more time to focus on customer needs and thus make more money for the company. Still, Anixter's top management wanted some assurance that the new training helped people become more productive more quickly than before and that the corporation's core values were being instilled.

That old bugaboo, measurement, often rears its ugly head when these issues arise. Anixter attempts to measure the impact of electronic training in a number of ways. Perhaps the most obvious and important way is linking the training to sales figures—are the systems helping people sell more? The managers also try to determine whether this electronic training system is increasing the appeal of the work environment to Anixter's employees and decreasing turnover. On the most basic level, Anixter's training people are assessing whether trainees can get through the software and what they get out of it. And on a grassroots level, the company is soliciting feedback to determine how individuals feel about the systems' efficacy.

The topic of measurement leads me to one of those stories that answers the value question better than anything else can. The head of Anixter's operation in Australia was a highly successful entrepreneur, the type of person who took little on faith and trusted implicitly in his own gut instincts. *Skepticism* might be too mild a word to describe his reaction when he heard about computerized simulations that encouraged failure as a catalyst for skill acquisition. Yet when he actually began interacting with the simulation, his voice boomed through the hallways as he shouted for various people to come in and see what he was doing. "This ain't philosophy," he roared in approval. "This is a deliverable."

That doesn't mean that Anixter has removed all the kinks from its systems. Though the new training has been very well received, Anixter still asks questions about it: Is it helping new people acquire skills more rapidly? Can it be updated constantly? Can we find the best way to use it in our culture? How much will it help the culture become self-renewing?

Those are all good questions, and ones that Anixter will answer with the experience practice brings.

THE RIGHT PERSPECTIVE FOR VIRTUAL LEARNING

Some cultures may not be as attuned to this training approach as others. Some organizations believe strongly in learning by telling; they don't like to hear the word *failure* spoken; they don't believe in investing much money in training, preferring to hire expertise or let people learn through trial and error.

Anixter's culture, on the other hand, is ideally suited to this new learning approach. Let's look at some of the cultural elements that make it so:

- **High value on expertise**. The people who do well at Anixter are those who have the most expertise. Mastery of skills is esteemed throughout the organization. This cultural trait motivates users to learn from goal-based scenarios; it gives learners a good reason to take the scenarios seriously and work hard at them.

- **Conversation and storytelling as the forms of communication**. Anixter people have always been great storytellers and conversationalists. From the day the company was founded, this has been the method by which expertise has been passed on. It was an easy jump for them when the ILS team began designing systems around stories.

- **An acceptance of failure as part of the process**. Again, note here that Anixter does not have a defeatist attitude nor does it accept bad quarters happily. What the managers do accept is that expectation failure happens—people expect one outcome and are shocked to discover another outcome entirely. Anixter recognizes that this failure produces prime teachable moments, and the company therefore embraced the idea of simulating experiences that lead to these moments.
- **Fun is good**. Anixter does not take a monastic approach to its work. The employees are not deadly serious every moment of every day. The company's culture is open and informal; it derides pomposity and encourages people to enjoy themselves at work. This attitude carries over to training. The humor and entertainment that facilitate learning were easy for Anixter to accept.

Julie Anixter sums it up best when she describes the link between the company's culture and the new electronic learning systems: "We want to keep our culture alive. It differentiates us to our customers and to ourselves. We view these systems as a beautiful solution to keep a vibrant sales culture alive, enhanced, and spreading throughout the world."

9
CHAPTER

Target and Bennigans Say, No More Mindless Robots

The last few chapters have focused on organizations that want to teach relatively sophisticated skills to bright, college-educated employees eager to do well at their chosen careers. Other organizations, however, are more concerned about another group of workers and skills. These firms want to teach "people" skills to the employee who may never have gone to college. They want to train the customer service technician, waitress, store clerk, and anyone else who interacts with the public; the companies want to train this employee to deal with people empathetically, knowledgeably, and innovatively.

Such companies recognize that in a service economy, the only thing that will differentiate them from competitors is people skills. When most organizations are offering basically the same product at basically the same price, quality of service is where they can gain the competitive edge. Put another way: Customers will give their business to the companies with the most helpful employees.

At least I will. I recently stayed at an elegant New York hotel, and when I made the reservation, I asked for a quiet room far away from the elevator. When I arrived, my room was in a noisy location next to the elevator. When I called the desk and asked for another room, the hotel clerk was indifferent. When I repeated my request, she sighed and said, "Well, I suppose I might be able to find something, though of course we'll be charging you a higher rate."

Interestingly, when I arrived in my room (before I complained) it contained a bottle of wine, compliments of the hotel. This was a nice gift, but it's one that every guest receives. Like many organizations, the hotel finds this type of "routine" customer service easy to provide. Problems arise when the routine no longer suffices—when employees are confronted with situations they're not prepared for. The hotel has only trained people in the policies and rules; it never readied them to think on their feet and consider the needs of individual guests. As this chapter shows, there's a reason why training in serving the public all assumes that customers are exactly alike and the standard policies will cover every situation.

TARGET EMPLOYEES ARE NATURALLY SMART

Recall a recent interaction with a customer service representative—a hotel reservations clerk, a rental car clerk, your doctor's receptionist, or a retail salesperson. The odds are that you've had some frustrating, unpleasant interactions. Perhaps you wanted to return something but were refused or humiliated during the process. Maybe you wanted to get some information and were treated like you were asking for the combination to the corporate safe. Or it could be that you came away from an interaction feeling like the other person had about as much personality and warmth as a piece of lint.

It's easy to assume that the people you're dealing with are cretins; it's the assumption behind a lot of the bad training that's out there.

Overcoming Previous Educational Experiences

Target doesn't hire Harvard MBAs to staff customer complaint desks, nor does Bennigans for its bartending positions. But the people these organizations hire aren't "dumb." Some of these employees, however, didn't do well in school. The problem may have been that such employees grew up in environments that made it difficult for them to concentrate in school; they were distracted by poverty, hunger, gangs, and so on. Or the employees may have had other personal problems that caused them to goof off or nod off in school. Whatever the reason for their poor academic achievement, the vast majority of these people are reasonably intelligent.

By intelligent, I mean that such holders of "low-level" jobs do know how to perform complex tasks. These people have mastered an astonishing variety of skills, from driving a car to ordering food in a restaurant, to speaking English (and if you think learning English is easy, try teaching it to a computer). Thus, such adults are perfectly capable of acquiring and using the people skills necessary to establish good relationships with customers. They won't learn these skills, however, if the training *tells* them how to establish these relationships. Many of these people aren't good at doing what they're told; that's why they had problems in school. If, however, training puts them in scenarios where they can "do" without being told, they'll be much more likely to learn. Put them in simulated situations where they can fail in private and where they're motivated to acquire skills, and they'll pick up things fast.

But what if the people *are* dumb? Say that a certain percentage of people who are hired for customer service jobs are slow to learn, easily distracted, or are burdened with some type of learning disability. Even then, these employees can acquire key customer service skills if they're allowed to practice them. The script-based nature of thinking is why that last statement is so. Why do dumb people know how to get served quickly in a restaurant? Because they've been through that script time and again—they've practiced it to the point that they've mastered the skills involved. If training puts people through a script repeatedly (in ways that foster learning), this practice will lead to mastery.

Most training does the opposite, especially when the trainees aren't college graduates or the jobs are entry-level, customer service positions. The training programs attempt to teach trainees to memorize and follow specific principles and rules: "Here are the 10 steps to follow when a customer complains. . . ." Is it any wonder that so many customer service representatives act like robots? When the employees blindly follow "the rules," they lose the ability to interact with people on a human level.

Have you ever been in a situation where you made a simple and sensible request, and a customer service person responded by saying: *"I can't do that because of our policy."*

This employee memorized the policy and forgot what it's like to be human and on the receiving end of such treatment. The human response would be: *"What you're saying makes sense. We have a policy that says I shouldn't do that, but let me check with my supervisor, and if he says okay, I'll be glad to help you with your request."*

Certainly it's important for these employees to understand what the company's principles are and what policies they should follow. Rules are fine; following them with mindless obedience is what is so shortsighted.

Before describing Target's and Bennigans' training, I can't resist one more point related to the smart people/dumb people argument. Some smart people may be able to understand an abstract explanation and translate it into appropriate behavior some of the time. In other words, you probably could tell Albert Einstein how to program a VCR and he could do it right the first time without the benefit of repeated attempts. A dumb person couldn't do that. On the other hand, smart people frequently can't do this trick of translating abstract explanations into corresponding behavior. Try giving a straight-A high school student a list of 20 rules about how to drive a car and see how long it takes before he crashes into a tree. If the written instruction approach doesn't work well with smart people, why use it with dumb people? It makes more sense to use an approach that works no matter what the learner's intelligence level is.

Rules Are Made to Be Broken

The Learning Sciences Corporation worked on diverse projects for Target stores. The first project was designed to help

Target's employees deal with an upcoming initiative designed to lower store costs by 2 percent. Anticipating numerous questions and concerns about the initiative, Target charged LSC with creating software that captured corporate memory and experts' stories related to cost-cutting, productivity, and related issues. The interactive computer format combined with employees' desire to know more about this timely subject (they were motivated to learn) made this a great success internally and encouraged Target to give LSC another assignment.

The simulation created by the LSC team was designed for service desks at Target stores—what most people refer to as the "complaint" desk. Target had been experiencing significant problems with people holding this position. The desk was staffed by employees who were not highly-paid and did not have advanced degrees, yet it's a crucial area for Target. The managers recognized that interactions took place at the desks that could make or break customer relationships: Handle a customer's problem well and you have established the basis for a long-term relationship; fail to solve it (or make it worse) and you have lost the customer. At the same time, these employees were often caught between policy and practice—between what the return policy dictated and what customers wanted. As you can imagine, the store's return policy did not always satisfy customers, who felt the policy shouldn't apply to their particular situation. Training customer service people to develop problem-solving skills, therefore, was a priority. Target managers reasoned that those skills included knowing how to calm down angry customers, bend store policy, and elicit information from customers about their problem that would help meet their needs.

The LSC simulation contains eight scenarios that mirror real service desk situations. One scenario, for instance, begins with a videotape of a guy attempting to return a pair of used sneakers that he bought four months ago, claiming "they're junk." From the appearance of the sneakers, the employee could easily conclude that they've just fallen apart from long, hard use. Still, the customer insists they're defective and wants his money back.

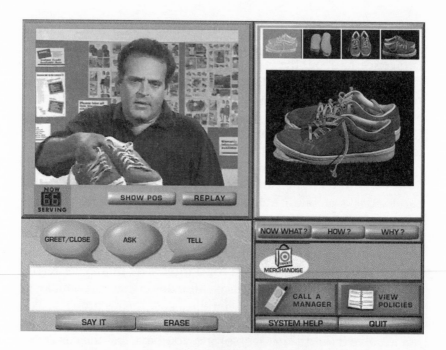

Four months is beyond the time frame allowed by Target's standard return policy. As a result, most trainees refuse to give the man his money back, are discourteous to him, or they start grilling him about how his shoes became so worn.

In other words, the trainees have many options in this simulation for experiencing expectation failure. A tutoring system is activated by these failures, and stories are told to demonstrate what trainees are doing wrong and how they might handle the situation differently.

Target wants to train employees to use their judgment and recognize what to do when goals conflict (the goal of following policy versus the goal of treating a customer like "a guest"). The trainers are *not* teaching people to ignore policy; they're helping them recognize when it makes sense to invoke it and when it makes no sense at all.

The simulation creates a series of common situations and offers trainees many chances to make the wrong decision or say the wrong things to customers. Trainees are surprised when the tutoring program is activated and corrects them. Expectation failure occurs a number of times in the simulation, giving rise to the most teachable moments there are. Here's a sampling of some common failures:

- Not greeting the customer properly (in a polite and respectful manner).
- Responding in kind to an angry customer (with a line of customers, the trainee helps someone who lacks a number, prompting someone with a number to belligerently inquire why Target has a number system if it doesn't use it).
- Insulting or demeaning someone who lacks a recent receipt (implying the receipt looks suspicious, for instance).
- Suggesting a product exchange when the customer wants cash back.
- Being overly aggressive when the employee suspects the customer is returning something not purchased at Target.

Target's training program is revolutionary not only because it features computer simulations but also because it teaches people to recognize that policy isn't written in stone. Many trainees have been taught the opposite tact by school and other employers. If they didn't follow the rules in school or policies at work, they were reprimanded, suspended, and fired. No one taught them what to do when there was an exception to the rules, when policy didn't apply. Target wants its people to substitute common sense and initiative for mindless adherence to policy in these situations—a stance that is eminently reasonable and somewhat radical.

What's also radical is that Target's training makes learning fun. Training for customer service jobs tends to be as dull as dull can be. At least some of the training for higher-level positions feature speakers who are provocative or involve people climbing mountains or surviving in the wilderness. Customer service trainees are viewed in much the same way that schools view below-average students; teachers believe the only way such students absorb a lesson is if the teachers go slowly, repeating information a lot and testing constantly to make sure students are doing the work. Customer service training sessions at most organizations are like attending the most basic high school English lecture; it's a struggle to stay awake let alone to learn. Target's computer simulation is fun because the actors ham it up and create "difficult customer" characters that every trainee knows well. It's fun to try different behaviors to deal with those customers and find the one that works.

According to Target's Deb Larsen, who manages these training projects, people really enjoy the expert tutoring aspect of the simulation. When trainees made mistakes in school or at other jobs, they usually were mentally beaten up for their errors, received a lecture, or no one cared. But the simulation's tutor responds in a number of different ways, depending on the mistake made or the type of help requested by the trainee.

One way the tutor responds is with relevant stories. Trainees find it remarkably easy to translate the knowledge gained from the stories into decisions that correct the mistakes they previously made.

At the time of this writing, Target was still in the process of deploying the virtual learning simulations throughout the retail system. The testing phase went so well that corporate leaders have requested a new series of simulations to become part of the company's executive training. If virtual learning works for the lower-paid, less educated employees, why shouldn't it work for higher-paid, more educated ones?

BENNIGANS SHOWS CUSTOMERS ITS IRISH HOSPITALITY

On one level, the Bennigans restaurant chain wanted to train its bartenders to do the impossible: Tell customers anything they wanted to know about 300 beers. As a goal of the computer simulation that an LSC team created for the barpeople, this was woven into the larger goal of helping bartenders treat customers as guests. This larger objective meant that bartenders couldn't just learn about all the beers and then say to a customer, "Hey, buddy, you don't want a Bud, we got 300 beers here and I know everything there is to know about each one of 'em." The idea was for the bartenders to get into the spirit of the promotion and the company; to learn to sell in a way that was both fun and knowledgeable. Bennigans managers wanted their people to be comfortable communicating with customers about the beer selection and other matters.

A big impetus toward doing this via a computer simulation was the age of Bennigans' managers and bartenders. They are relatively young people who have grown up with computers; most of them are not big manual readers. The managers and bartender trainees alike enjoy the challenge of computer games and aren't timid about venturing into virtual world scenarios. Brad Lutz and Susie Sciolino, the two training executives who brought the LSC team into Bennigans, recognized early on that this was the way the training should go. After talking with them, I was able to identify what was wrong with their past training: It taught their managers to be "fry guys" when the restaurant became crowded, to start cooking when they should be managing; it forced them to memorize procedures and rules rather than help them learn how to deal with common managerial situations. As a result, Brad and Susie pushed hard for our virtual learning approach, and after months of pushing (and hearing objections related to budgets), they finally received approval to bring the team in.

Using Expectation Failure Wisely

Like the Target simulation, Bennigans' program begins by inviting trainees into a virtual world in which a customer approaches (in a videotaped clip). It leads the bartenders into customer dialogues and situations where trainees experience expectation failure after expectation failure. When they fail by saying or doing the wrong thing, the program stops them and tells a story that illustrates the problem and how it might be solved.

When I tried the program for the first time, I instinctively started by asking the customer, "What would you like to drink?" That seems like a logical opening question for a bartender to ask a customer. Not at Bennigans. The program stopped me and explained how I had failed to introduce myself.

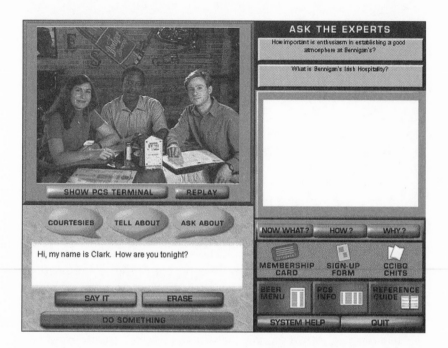

Trainees frequently make the following mistakes:

- Failing to ask customers how they're doing, what's happening, and so on.
- Failing to inquire whether customers are members of Bennigans' special beer club.
- Failing to ask for an I.D. when appropriate.
- Failing to thank customers for showing the I.D., for being a member of the club, and so on.

All the coaching and stories in the world aren't going to turn an innately sullen and obnoxious bartender into a charming character. But Bennigans is correct in assuming that's not the transformation that has to be made. Most bartenders choose their profession because they like talking to and being with other people and are good at it. The computer simulation is designed to help them channel their friendliness to meet Bennigans' customer service goals. Another restaurant, for instance, might define friendliness as nothing more than a smile and a hello; Bennigans takes the interaction to a different level.

At the same time, the program motivates bartenders to learn about the 300 beers. One of the ways it does so is by having a customer ask the bartender a question such as, "What is a pilsner?" when one is the beer of the month. Naturally, the bartender is embarrassed not to know the answer. If the trainee takes any pride in this profession, he or she doesn't want to be embarrassed like that again. Because this is a private failure, the trainee doesn't become so angry, defensive, or depressed that the learning impulse is snuffed out. The privacy of a computer simulation enables the bartender to rebound from his or her failure by examining what went wrong and what to do differently the next time. The virtual learner is able to take advantage of the program's explanations of what a pilsner is and become forearmed with this knowledge. Throughout the program, the trainee can explore everything from how a porter is made to the history of lager beer.

Practice Makes the Bartender Knowledgeable

One experience with the program probably won't do it. Ideally, Bennigans' bartenders will practice with the program until friendliness and knowledge become second nature. Right now, it looks like they're practicing quite a bit. In Bennigans' four highest-volume restaurants, the computer simulations are being used repeatedly by staff.

They use it because it's fun to challenge themselves with the goal-based scenarios, and they also rely on it to obtain just-in-time knowledge. If a bartender is hearing questions about porter or stout, for example, he or she can access stories and information about that beer category and respond intelligently to customer inquiries. In other words, bartenders can use the computer simulation in multiple ways.

THE MOST IMPORTANT PEOPLE SKILLS

There's another way to categorize the people skills organizations like Target and Bennigans are teaching. Although the overall goal is to help their customer service people be more friendly, respectful, helpful, and empathetic, specific skills allow them to achieve this goal.

The first is *listening*. One of the shocks to trainees during computer simulations is when trainees realize they didn't really hear what the customer said. They jump to conclusions, make false inferences, and hear only part of what the customer actually said. It may be that they've dealt with a lot of angry customers recently, and the trainees' mood and mindset makes them predisposed to hear the negative. Or they're so busy that they don't take the time and concentrate on the information someone is requesting. People don't learn how to listen until they're jarred into recognizing this failure. The simulations do exactly that. Trainees expect that they've heard a customer correctly and are surprised to find they did not. Expectation failure opens their minds to learning.

The second skill is *being accommodating*. This refers not only to politeness (though nothing vexes a customer like a rude salesperson) but also to responsiveness to customer needs. Bennigans and Target want their people to feel that it's their personal responsibility to satisfy customer complaints and requests. These companies want them to care about doing so. Certainly the simulations can alert trainees to situations where they're not accommodating but thought they were being helpful. But training alone can't do it all. It helps if a rewards system is in place that motivates people to take personal responsibility for satisfying customer complaints.

The third skill is one mentioned before but one that deserves a bit more description here: *Thinking on your feet*. This skill translates into everything from creativity to problem-solving. The ability to make quick, satisfactory solutions are what enables an employee to deal with a situation that varies from the norm. This ability is what enables a Target employee to ignore store policy and offer a refund if it makes sense or a Bennigans bartender to suggest just the right alternative selection when a customer says he likes stout but thinks the beer of the month tastes like contaminated sewer water.

In one simulation, a customer starts yelling at the store employee. The employee who can't think on his feet responds with what the manual says to do in this situation: "Tell irate customer to calm down." Or he responds as he would in a similar personal situation—when he and his spouse are having a fight—and yells back. Using the simulation, trainees can also respond to yelling customers in these ways but have the opportunity to try more productive responses. It takes a while for trainees to discover the "think-on-your-feet" way: Discerning why the customer is upset and then dealing with the real issue (for example, a customer comes in screaming about a spot in the dress she bought and what she's *really* angry about is that the dress is a size too small).

Traditional training asks employees to memorize the script, but it doesn't tell them what to do when the customer departs from the script. You can witness this rote behavior all the time— not just on planes, in stores, or at hotels, but in teaching and working with your own employees. A little while back, the Andersen Consulting people trained at Northwestern came up with new software designs, and I didn't like any of them. They returned a week later with the same designs modified a bit. I still didn't like them. "Tell us why you don't like them," they demanded. I suggested that they analyze it themselves and determine what if anything was wrong with the designs. If I *told* them what was wrong, they'd simply make a list and modify their original, unacceptable ideas to be not quite as bad. When the Andersen team analyzed the designs themselves, they came up with much better ideas. They were thinking on their feet, not relying on the "script" according to Schank or anyone else.

Most employees can't or won't think for themselves because they're the products of an educational system that teaches: "Do what you're told; don't venture a risky guess or a provocative opinion. Give us the answer we want rather than the answer you want to give." The creative impulse is squeezed out of people after years of such teaching. Schools pretend the world is an objective place with right answers and right ways of doing things. In fact, it's a subjective place with lots of ambiguity. The simulations described here for Bennigans and Target help trainees understand that there are *various* right answers; that there are alternative paths through the program. Of course, virtual learning simulations reveal certain parameters of appropriate and inappropriate behaviors. But within these boundaries, employees are encouraged to take risks and rely on their instinct and initiative. If they practice thinking on their feet enough times, most of them will get the hang of it despite all the time spent in school thinking on another part of their anatomy.

TWO BIG OBSTACLES

Why do relatively few employees in service industries possess people skills? Two reasons come to mind:

- Schools are too busy teaching "more important" things.
- Organizations that are doing well don't see the need to polish the service they offer.

Schools maintain that it's important to concentrate on teaching algebra, chemistry, state capitals, and mediocre 17th-century poems. But wouldn't it be much more advantageous for students and society if students learned how to empathize, manage, reason, sell, and make decisions? Such life skills are usually missing from education. Everyone becomes upset when a study is published claiming that U.S. science and math scores have gone down while scores in other nations have gone up. So what? I'd be much more concerned if a study showed that our people skills scores had plummeted. The majority of students will find little use after graduation for all the math and science facts they tried to cram into their heads. On the other hand, most students will have great use for the people skills they should have been taught.

Not that every organization will allow its staff to use those skills. Some companies aren't particularly visionary when it comes to their service policies. The airlines are a good example.

Most of the ones remaining (after the bankruptcies and acquisitions) are fat and sassy; they're flying full planes most of the time and aren't overly concerned with individualizing services to customers. That's why you hear those incredibly irritating loud-speaker announcements of gates for every conceivable connecting flight. The announcements are hard to hear, they are often subject to change, the information is easy to forget, and monitors all over the airport provide the same information in a much more friendly and accessible way. The policy doesn't consider that the announcements might drive customers a little nutty. Similarly, airlines insult our intelligence with what I call "do-do" speak: "We do request that you do fasten your seatbelts." Would you bet that helping verbs are a component of their customer policy?

In time these organizations will realize this policy hurts the bottom line. LSC's clients tend to come from highly competitive industries; they recognize that an enlightened service policy is crucial if they expect to maintain and expand their customer base. They also understand that they can train their service people to be more than the mindless robots who (intentionally or not) irritate, aggravate, and antagonize.

MOVING FORWARD

Having read about the virtual learning that's taking place at Bennigans, Target, Diamond, Anixter, and Andersen, you may have a number of "how-do-I-sell-this-to-my-boss" questions. Probably the easiest way—and one alluded to earlier—is by focusing on the cost and time savings of virtual learning. Another way, however, is by communicating that this is a more effective way to train employees. The concluding four chapters should arm you for discussing its effectiveness. They will give you a number of stories to tell about the techniques that enhance goal-based scenarios' efficacy. These chapters will also give you a preview of a virtual learning future. And Chapter 10 provides this good argument for virtual learning in training: It's designed to work in harmony with the way the mind learns.

10
CHAPTER

THE WAY THE MIND WORKS, THE WAY TRAINING SHOULD

You don't have to be a psychologist to create effective training, but it helps to have some understanding of how the mind does its magic trick of storing and retrieving information. At the very least, this understanding will help you become more comfortable with the notion of virtual learning.

This chapter doesn't describe in boring scientific detail how our minds work (then you'd be sure to forget it). It does, however, give you a sense of why we remember certain things and not others. This is important, if only because one of the most common complaints in organizations is, "He didn't remember a single thing he learned in training."

Maybe it's because he never learned it.

Schools and organizations make a faulty assumption: If it's taught clearly and if people are tested on it, it will be remembered. In fact, clarity and testing have little to do with whether something is remembered.

Think about what you remember from your own life—your first date; a loved one's death; being fired from a job; your wedding. We recall best what impacts us the most. You may have studied like a crazy person to pass a geography test; you may have memorized the locations of towns, rivers, and mountain ranges until you were sure you would never forget them. But of course you forgot them. Unless you practiced knowing where these places were, experienced some emotional event in one of these places, or had a goal for remembering where they were 20 years later, the odds are you couldn't find the Yalu River on a map if your life depended on it.

Why is it that most people who are older than 40 can remember exactly what they were doing when they heard about President Kennedy's assassination? The emotional wallop of a president's murder plays a role. But it's the completely unexpected nature of the event that branded it in our brains. This was expectation failure to the nth degree. The last thing anyone expected was that the president would be shot. Most Americans were thrown into a state of confusion when we heard the news. Virtual learning aims to produce a similar—if somewhat less catastrophic—effect in training.

VIOLATING THE SCRIPT

People have a "script" in their heads for just about everything. The script is their expectation of how a certain event will unfold. For instance, the airplane script in most passengers' heads involves expectations about buying a ticket, waiting at the gate to board, handing the gate attendant a boarding pass, finding the seat, and so on. That script would be violated if passengers find the pilot sprawled out in the aisle drinking from a whiskey bottle. When this expectation failure occurs, passengers are not likely to forget it.

Now let's try a more sophisticated example that involves a subject near and dear to my heart. You're walking down the street with a friend who suggests going to a restaurant. You agree that you'd like to eat, and your friend takes you into Burger King. Assume for the sake of this story that you've never eaten at or even heard about a fast-food restaurant. When you go into Burger King, the service fails to meet the expectations generated by your restaurant script. No one seats you; no one hands you a menu; you have to pay before rather than after you've eaten. These failures are memorable.

The next day, you go to McDonald's. You of course notice its similarities to Burger King; you experience the same expectation failures; one experience reminds you of another. You create a new set of expectations in your mind and label them the *fast-food script*.

This is learning. In this process, you have a set of expectations; they fail to be realized; you remember other experiences in which you failed in the same way; and you create a new set of expectations.

Trainers want to do the same thing in training. The ideal training scenario creates great confusion; trainees will be surprised, shocked, and otherwise flabbergasted at how things aren't going according to plan. People will fail to complete a task or meet a goal, but they won't fail in anticipated ways. Instead, they'll do something that really screws up the works. Remember how ridiculous Andersen's Zed restaurant was because of people's failures. Or how trainees using Anixter's scenarios often receive a memorable chewing out because they failed to include a Lucent representative in the sales process.

Failing in interesting ways should be a goal of training. Training through virtual learning should systematically (though artfully) lead people toward the proverbial cliff, unaware of where they're going until they find themselves falling. Many trainers resist this path. When I tried a flight simulator and managed to crash the plane, I was told I was the first one ever to do so. If I were in charge of training pilots, I would make *sure* to fashion a scenario in which trainees had to navigate through severe lightning with one engine out and the others sputtering, the cabin filling with smoke, and the plane being tossed about. Better to have pilots experience this situation as a simulation than as they fly a real plane. Then if such a catastrophe happens in the air, the pilot will be reminded of the simulator experience (in which the pilot probably did something wrong and crashed) and know what *not* to do.

It's hard for companies to grasp the notion of safe failure. Telling an organization that its training should encourage people to make horrendous mistakes can rub managers the wrong way. An analogy to learning how to drive a car can help reluctant CEOs to understand. Besides the largely perfunctory driver's education courses offered by school, teenagers learn to drive by almost killing themselves and others. New drivers fail in all sorts of interesting and truly memorable ways, and there's no question that if they survive the accidents and close calls, they become better drivers. Companies allow their new, inexperienced employees to have similarly horrific accidents on the job. If the employees aren't fired for incompetence, they probably grow to become skilled employees.

Building expectation failure into the training process is an alternative to this school of hard knocks.

The other consideration for organizations is that when employees know only one script, they aren't particularly adaptable. If all that training has taught them is the company-approved way to perform their job, they'll be completely lost when the job doesn't go according to the script. At a time when change is omnipresent in the work world, it makes sense to let workers experience a script failure during training. Out of this failure, they can learn to create a new script and adjust when things don't go exactly as planned.

THE MIND AND THE COMPUTER

Why do companies even need computer simulations to implement this learning process? It's a question that occurs to many organizations that view role-playing as simpler, faster, and less expensive. Certainly role-playing is all of these things. Computers, however, are much more learning-friendly; they provide an environment that is more conducive to learning than a role-playing scenario.

Earlier you read about Diamond's and Andersen's role-playing techniques, and both those organizations have obviously benefited from them. I've also pointed out the main drawback of role-playing—people don't like to fail in front of others, and without failure, there is no learning. Diamond and Andersen have been clever about the scenarios they've created, and they've avoided some of the learning problems that come with live scenarios.

Other companies haven't been so lucky. The trend in organizations toward group learning and project teams ignores a fundamental principle of how our minds work: *Our ability to label and store a failure for later use is diminished by the embarrassment, humiliation, blaming, and anger that accompany a public failure.*

Think about what happens when you mess up in front of a group. Say you've just completed a presentation, and your boss remarks negatively about the quality of your ideas. If you're like most people, you'll respond one of two ways:

- **Blame the boss for your failure**. When an employee fails, he or she needs to explain that failure. Learning doesn't take place in this instance because the employee becomes convinced that the failure was the boss's fault. Rather than focusing on what he or she did wrong and storing it for future reference, the employee remembers blame and anger.

- **Blame yourself and feel embarrassed and humiliated**. Memory of an experience is corrupted by strong negative emotions. The valuable lessons associated with failure aren't stored whole; the employee becomes so upset that it overwhelms his or her mind's capacity to label and store.

When role-playing scenarios are constructed cleverly, the mind may be "tricked" and the blaming responses circumvented. Recall that Diamond found that role-playing worked wonderfully when a team was fired by the "CEO"; the shock of being fired would not soon be forgotten and the trainees wouldn't get fired in a real consulting engagement. Perhaps the blaming response was avoided because the entire team failed together—an individual wasn't scapegoated. Perhaps it was avoided because the Diamond culture encourages risk-taking and failure, and what would have been humiliating in another culture was acceptable here.

Trainees' reactions all reflect their motivation in training. If a company takes *all* the sting out of failure, it won't be memorable. If people view the failure as trivial or they don't have much of a vested interest in succeeding, the role-playing scenario won't stick. The motivation isn't there for the trainees' unconscious to file it in a properly labeled drawer. Of course, if failure goes too far in the other direction and feels like the end of the world, blaming starts.

Failing during a computer simulation, on the other hand, usually doesn't trigger our blaming impulse (of course, some people might blame the software for being too difficult or unfair, but that's the exception). The computer simulation offers three distinct advantages:

- **The failure is private**. Though learners may feel like idiots when they mess up an assigned task or become unhappy when a supervisor appears on the screen and explains they were wrong in their approach, people's feelings are cushioned because there's no one around to observe the failure. This cushion enables memory to do its label-and-store number.

- **The failure can be explained by experts**. When learners make blunders, their minds cry out for explanation. At that moment especially, trainees are open to suggestions. It's what the psychologists call a "teachable moment." In real life or in role-playing, people may be too upset to listen to an expert's advice. Or the advice may come days later, when learners are far past that teachable moment. In a computer simulation, the expert is programmed to appear *right when* people fail.

- **The failure can be controlled**. In real life, humans fail by accident. They don't plan to fail in exactly the right way so to maximize learning. Sometimes novices fail at an esoteric task and the knowledge gained from that failure will never be needed again. In role-playing, too, the failure can be random. Diamond didn't script the firing of its team; it was just a fortuitous event. Trainers can design computer simulation failures so that the focus is on learning targeted skills.

The other issue involves teams. Because team skills have become so critical to organizations, many companies feel that the training should take place in teams. Although this logic may be sound, its implementation is flawed. People don't like to fail with their peers watching; the team skills they should be learning are not sinking in because of the powerful negative emotions that arise during a humiliating performance. In a computer simulation, people can have "virtual teammates." In fact, the trainer can program each teammate for the common personality traits a given trainee has the most problems with. If, for instance, John has trouble dealing with aggressive, assertive team members, that's exactly the type of person John's trainer wants to program into the software. In a typical team training situation, the trainer would be stuck with the randomness factor—the four or five people on John's team may not be the right mix for him (they may all be the type of people he naturally works well with), nor may his personality facilitate their learning.

STORING, LABELING, AND RETRIEVING MOMENTS

Throughout, this chapter has referred to the way the mind labels and stores information. Now you're ready to explore the mechanics of this process in a bit more detail so you'll understand how ILS attempts to replicate this process in our goal-based scenarios.

What did you do on your last vacation? What's the worst thing that ever happened to you at work? You automatically think of relevant stories when you hear these questions. Your mind has a retrieval mechanism that unconsciously searches and finds the right stories. But how? Consider the story of the steak and the haircut.

My ex-wife never made steak the way I liked it. She always cooked the thing to death and beyond, and I enjoy my steak rare. I was complaining to a friend about my then-wife's unfortunate tendency to overcook meat, and he replied, "I couldn't get my hair cut as short as I wanted." Although his response might seem like a nonsequitor, it was actually almost identical to my story—at least at a certain level of abstraction. Unconsciously, my friend labeled my story as "extreme." In other words, my wife's overcooking was an extreme or my desire for rare meat was an extreme. On an abstract level, he was labeling his desire for a short haircut as extreme. And in both his case and mine, we were unable to achieve our extreme goals. He sent my story out to memory and what came back was his story.

It's important to understand that levels of abstraction are in terms of failures, goals, plans, and difficulties of achieving plans. In my friend's mind, we each failed to achieve an extreme goal.

If you're confused by the concept of level of abstraction, think about proverbs. For instance, an old Jewish proverb is: *If you dance at every wedding, you'll cry at every funeral.* In other words, if your goal is to have fun through relationships with other people, your goal will be thwarted because all those people will eventually die and you'll be spending your time mourning. The language of goals is abstracted here, and it's the same language our minds use to store and retrieve memories.

From a training standpoint, therefore, it's not sufficient to just give trainees useful experiences. Training needs to offer experiences that learners can store and label properly. If a trainer tells trainees about how they should work in teams, they will acquire an experience of sorts, but they will lack the goals and plans necessary for the mind to store it and retrieve it from memory. Virtual learning scenarios—especially those constructed expertly on computers—use goals and plans so that memories can be stored at the proper level of abstraction. When Tina fails to list the right requirements for a system, the system fails, and that goal failure translates to a level of abstraction that she'll retrieve and use at some point in the future—at the point that an experience conjures up the same label at the same level of abstraction.

KEEPING CERTAIN PRINCIPLES IN MIND

Training is ineffective when it doesn't consider the ways people learn. This chapter has mentioned some of the principles of how the mind works. Now take a look at three common ways training violates those principles:

- **Dullness.** Even many professors who teach by telling recognize that if they want their students to remember even a small piece of the lecture, they had better do something out of the ordinary. Examples include the chemistry professor who blows up something in the lab to make a point, the sociology professor who tells an emotionally wrenching story about a client, and the political science professor who outrages everyone with a politically incorrect story. Training is often unconscionably dull. The lecture material, the delivery, and the workbooks all could knock an insomniac out in seconds flat. Horrify, stun, amuse, offend—do *something* worthy of being remembered.

- **Unreal situations.** The memory has trouble storing that which it knows to be a fabrication. The worst role-playing scenarios are ones that employees laugh at behind the trainer's back, the ones that set up situations that couldn't possibly happen in the real world of work. A lot of team training commits this sin—people know that real team environments are much more volatile and unstructured than those in training sessions. LSC's scenarios always guard against scripting fake realities. In one coaching module, a scene called for a subordinate talking to someone two levels up from him about golfing together. It was completely unrealistic or at least rare for a junior executive and a middle manager to socialize in this way. Even minor flaws such as this one can cause people to reject the scenario and thus fail to store and label it properly.

- **Bad timing.** Training often dictates that masses of people go to a given classroom at a given time and receive instruction in a particular topic. It does not allow for the fact that many people won't need to use the information for days, weeks, or months. It's ironic that even much of the ballyhooed multimedia training is done this way. Rather than take advantage of a software-based system's flexibility, organizations revert to the educational model: Everyone must complete x hours of training before going on; the learner must make it through every second of the computer program before being allowed to put the knowledge to use. This regimentation forces companies to lock into training schedules. The way learning should be done is just-in-time. The mind can only hold so much information for so long—when there's a lot of data, it should be conveyed just before it's needed. Even more important, people need to be motivated to learn. If learners know they're not going to use the training information for months, learners won't have much of an incentive to concentrate. If, on the other hand, learners have a sales meeting with a lawyer tomorrow—and they screwed up the last presentation to a lawyer—they'll concentrate intently on training that occurs just before tomorrow's meeting.

NATURAL LEARNING VERSUS TRAINING

Training is often a knee-jerk response. Organization leaders see a skill their staff lacks or an area where people need more knowledge and the managers automatically turn to training. The amount of unnecessary training that goes on in companies today is staggering.

Perhaps the most egregious examples of this practice involve computer training. Companies routinely spend millions of dollars and thousands of work hours helping their people learn how to master new software—spreadsheet, word processing, and other common computer functions. Such training is a waste of time and money for three reasons:

- People's minds can't absorb the avalanche of information that typically comes with these courses—trainers can drill people like demons and trainees still won't correctly label and store 57 commands for future use.

- Because the systems are new, there's no body of experience and expertise to draw on. Without the knowledge of where the failures are likely to take place and what might be done to avoid them, learning won't happen. It will only happen when trainers lead people into the places where they're most likely to fail on the job—when training does that, the unconscious mind gets interested and remembers.

- Most importantly, this training is unnecessary because people will learn how to use the software on their own. Natural learning—the process by which people fail and practice and fail and practice until they get it right— makes sense in instances like these:
  —When a system or process is new and there's no available expertise or experience with which to structure training.
  —When there's time for people to learn on their own and they can fail without any significant, negative consequences for the organization.
  —When a de facto apprenticeship process is in place to help people gain the job skills they need over time.

The head of a shipping company for whom LSC has designed systems called recently requesting help. After discussing his situation, I suggested that he didn't need new training systems and that the apprenticeship approach to training would work for him. On a boat, novice sailors have the time to ask questions and look over more experienced seamen's shoulders. Because of the close quarters and culture of learning on a ship, it's easy to learn from the experts. And there are plenty of mechanisms in place to ensure that a neophyte's mistake doesn't blow up the ship.

In the right situations and given enough time, people are great learners. It's true that sometimes organizations don't have the time to recoup from novices' mistakes. This same ship owner was concerned when new shipping regulations had been issued and his people had to learn them; the natural apprenticeship system wouldn't let them master the regulations quickly enough. Computer simulations can jump-start the apprenticeship process; the programs can concentrate the learning and condense the amount of time required to learn. Institute members have found that people's minds are able to accelerate the process of labeling and storing their stories. When time is a critical factor, training may be preferable to letting people learn on their own.

One final point about this issue remains: Some skills are easier for people to learn through training than others. Right now the training industry is witnessing a proliferation of training courses that revolve around leadership, diversity, teams, and coaching. It's not that these skills can't be taught; it just makes me nervous to try teaching them.

When LSC teams have built computer simulations and role-playing scenarios around these soft skills, people don't learn the skills as readily as skills pertaining to sales or widget-turning. Part of the problem is that it's difficult to define exactly what it is that makes a good leader or a good coach—or even what constitutes common failures in leadership and coaching.

The other part of the problem has to do with the inherent differences among people. We all learn the same way, but we're not all equally capable of learning the same things. Some people have the instinct and aptitude for leadership, for instance. Other people are naturally great communicators. Others are talented at facilitation.

You can't make a leader out of a follower, nor can you turn an intolerant individual into someone who values diversity. Even the best virtual learning can't implant talent or instinct. Organizations should recognize that some aspects of training are out of their control; that it makes sense to let leaders rise to the surface by adopting role models, mentoring, and developing their skills in "junior" leadership positions. Or they should think about how great communicators developed their abilities. They didn't take a training course and suddenly go out and give a brilliant speech. They started out giving awful speeches, learned from what they did wrong, and eventually reached the point where they could use their natural ability effectively.

Training can speed up this process if it takes into consideration the way the mind works and how learning really happens. That's the real magic of virtual learning scenarios. They don't turn people into something they're not, but they accelerate the process by which trainees become the employees they are capable of becoming.

11
CHAPTER

VIRTUAL LEARNING TECHNIQUES

To the uninitiated, creating a computer simulation seems extraordinarily difficult. Forgetting the technological challenges of this endeavor for the moment, there's the problem of getting people to tell useful stories and to tell them well; there's the scriptwriter's challenge of writing realistic scenes, and the filmmaker's task of translating the words into action; and finally, there's the instructor's trick of simulating interesting failures, providing multiple paths through the simulations, and ensuring the right mix of resources to help people get through the simulations.

No one claims this process is easy. However, any organization with a suitable skill to teach can create effective virtual learning, given the right tools and techniques. The tools are tough to describe. Though later the chapter briefly describes the tools LSC designers use to produce simulations for our clients, the tools are complex systems that have evolved for years. As the engines that power our simulations, they make this process affordable for our clients and enable us to work with relative dispatch.

This book doesn't break down these systems and tell you how to put them together yourself for three reasons:

- They're proprietary.
- It's boring to discuss—the system details won't excite anyone but a systems analyst.
- It's unnecessary. You can hire consultants like those at ILS or other programmers to develop these tools.

Techniques, however, comprise information that you should know about. To help learners master skills, designers and trainers should understand what constitutes a good story, how to formulate questions that elicit these stories, and how to script a realistic scenario. Again, you're not going to be able to *do* these things just by *reading* about them. But this chapter gives you techniques to practice or think about when your organization decides to create a simulation.

DESCRIPTION OF THE TECHNIQUES

Let's start by taking some of the mystery out of the simulation-creating process. Here's an overview of the process in chronological order of steps performed (the following is the process from LSC's perspective; if you are an in-house trainer or HR person, you can easily translate the steps to fit your situation):

1. **Meet with prospective client**. Sometimes corporate leaders come to us in crisis—they desperately need to train people in a skill in which the firms are in short supply. Maybe the companies have an expensive new computer system and no one understands how to use it. Perhaps the companies are driven by a competitive need—they need a skill that will help them gain a competitive edge. More often than not, organizations don't know *what* skill they want to teach. The managers simply say, "We spend a lot of money on training and we want to improve its effectiveness. Can you help us?"

2. **Obtain buy-in**. It's not always easy for companies to make the commitment to developing a computer simulation. Certainly there's the money issue—multimedia isn't cheap. But there are also psychological and emotional issues. People have to buy in to failure as a learning catalyst; into the idea that trainers can simulate reality on a computer; that trainers have to stop trying to tell people what companies want them to know.

3. **Pick a skill**. Once the buy-in is obtained, the ILS team starts working with companies to determine which skill to teach. Usually there are numerous choices and needs. Ultimately, the designers narrow down those choices to what is teachable—the skills in which companies have expertise and experience.

4. **Conduct interviews**. Next LSC team members interview employees, as much to obtain good stories as to understand what to teach. Asking the right questions is critical. In this step designers are searching for the common failures that can help people master targeted skills.

5. **Script (build the simulation)**. The challenge here is to hook the stories to the failures so that learning occurs and to do so in a realistic manner. If the simulation seems phony or people don't have access to stories that "explain" the failures, learning won't happen. Once all of the alternatives are scripted, it's simply a matter of putting everything together from a technological standpoint.

Virtual learning techniques make this process work. Let's examine some of them.

Asking the Right Questions

How do designers get people to tell the most useful failure-related stories? Imagine a company that wants to teach its people team-building skills. Designers start interviewing the company's team-building experts and find that the responses are not stories at all. A designer might ask, "Tell me about how you build a good cross-functional team" and the reply is, "We make sure every function is represented on the team, and we make sure that our team members understand the importance of diversity and communication." In other words, these interviewees pontificate for the camera rather than relating a story. Or they may tell a story, but it's a boring one or about something that isn't relevant to the skill the company wants to teach. The interviewer may even get people who are uncomfortable (for political or personal reasons) discussing failures; they prefer to talk about their successful use of a skill.

Guidelines for Story Gathering

To obtain the stories that are the foundation of effective virtual learning scenarios, here are some guidelines:

1. **Be specific.** Most people reflexively ask general, open-ended questions. Interviewers' tendency is to ask questions such as, "Tell me an interesting story that happened to you on the loading dock" or "What didn't work out for you in the past year when you were trying to make a sale?" Such an interviewer is much more likely to get a usable story by asking, "What caused the longest delay in loading a truck in the last year?" or "What's the worst mistake you made on a sales call that caused you to lose a customer?" Try an experiment. In a room of people, ask whether anyone has a story to tell about moving a refrigerator. Odds are that lots of them will remember one to tell, not because it's a story they tell frequently or because it's important to them, but because you've asked the question in a way that brings it readily to mind. Specificity doesn't always work at first, but if you ask enough specific questions, eventually it will.

2. **Get into the other person's indexing scheme**. What is an indexing scheme? It's nothing more than thinking about the way someone else stores and labels stories. When interviewers ask people for "interesting" experiences or "meaningful" contributions or "significant" achievements, interviewees will draw a blank. No one labels stories that way, so nothing comes to mind when these questions are asked. Interviewers are likely to cause them to retrieve a story by asking questions using the interviewee's language, even if that language seems foreign. I once interviewed a world expert in battle planning, who used terms that were completely divorced from my experience. Yet by constructing questions using his military jargon, I elicited great stories.

3. **Acquire domain knowledge**. Say a trainer is going to interview a poetry expert to learn what makes a poem great. Unfortunately, the trainer knows absolutely nothing about poetry. That interviewer is likely to end up asking this expert generic questions such as, "What makes for a great poem?" and "Who is your favorite poet and why is that poet so good?" Generic questions are the downfall of unknowledgeable interviewers. If the interviewer knew a bit about poetry, he or she might pose questions like, "Deconstruct 'Ode to a Grecian Urn' and tell me why it's a great poem" or "Why is a poet who writes such difficult and obscure verse like Ezra Pound considered great whereas a poet like Rod McKuen who writes such accessible poems considered a no-talent?" The point of all this is to learn something about an expert's field before an interviewer conducts an interview.

4. **Relate questions to likely failures**. People remember their failures. Or rather, if the interviewer asks a question in the right way, people will remember failures and tell them to the camera. Begin by simply thinking about all

the possible failures connected to a particular skill and build questions around them. Say a trainer is interviewing the world's leading authority on widget-turning (whatever that is). The trainer could pose questions such as:

- Was there ever a time a widget was turned so badly that it messed up production?
- Do you remember ever having to stop turning widgets because it became too expensive to do so?
- Was there a time that the apparatus you use to turn the widgets broke?
- Did the equipment break so badly that you had to find an alternative method to turn them?
- Did you ever turn a widget perfectly but the customer still rejected it?

You might not get a good failure story for each question, but you'll probably hit the jackpot with at least one of them.

5. **Throw in a question that compares apples and oranges**. For instance: Was there ever a time your widget-turning process resulted in a sexual harassment suit? The question seems nonsensical—what does sexual harassment have to do with turning widgets? Not much, on the surface. But deeper down in your expert's mind, it might trigger a story. Maybe it will jar the expert into remembering a story about how the widget-turning process generated some other unusual result: "Well, no, that would be kind of strange, but I remember when we put in a new procedure for turning widgets that called for us to work double shifts, and three of our workers got stressed out and one filed and won a lawsuit against the company." Sometimes it takes a juxtaposition of two unlikely topics to stir up a story.

6. **Help the storyteller to relax**. It's not easy to relax when a camera is trained at your head and you're being asked to recall a time when you or someone you work with

screwed up in spades. If you question people with all the finesse of a cop interrogating a suspect, you're not going to elicit much that is usable. Keeping your approach casual and conversational is just common sense. The ideal setting for your questions would be a friendly bar, and the ideal facilitator would be a bartender armed with free drinks. Because most companies would frown on this environment, your next best alternative is to be friendly. You might also want to ask people questions about their successes; they remember them almost as well as they recall their failures. Talking about a success is less threatening than explaining how they messed up, and it might help them relax enough to feel comfortable talking about a failure.

BUILDING REALISTIC SIMULATIONS

By definition, a simulation is one big step removed from reality. The trainer asks people to forget for a moment they're in front of a computer tapping on a keyboard and pretend that they're using a skill such as selling or coaching in a work environment. Amazingly, people are willing to suspend their disbelief. It's the same thing that happens when people go to a really good movie—it's so close to real life that they willingly pretend that it's actually happening. That's why good movies make us laugh and cry, why they keep us on the edge of our seat.

Simulations can evoke similar responses. The best ones create anxiety over a lost sale or confuse us because we don't understand how to complete a task. The worst ones evoke moans and groans of disbelief, cynical laughter, and complaints like, "No one would ever say that to a customer" or (sarcastically) "Yeah, I'm really going to solve a complex problem like that with one phone call." To produce realistic simulations (an oxymoron if ever there was one), here are some tips:

- **Simulate things the way they are, not how you wish they would be**. Sometimes discrepancies occur between what managers claim and what interviews of their people reveal. Corporate leaders make things seem better and easier than they are. One manager, for instance, wanted to portray customers in a simulation as being uniformly happy and accommodating. The employee interviews demonstrated that this was not the case; that a major problem was how to handle surly, overly demanding customers. The cognitive dissonance that results from managers insisting on a "separate reality" can fatally flaw the learning process.

- **Provide different paths through the simulation**. Simulations need to provide people with alternative ways to navigate through situations. Some learners ask a lot of questions in order to solve a problem, whereas others experiment with different approaches. If the designer creates a situation in which people must respond in a specific way in order to learn a skill, only those people who would naturally respond that way will learn it. Better simulations provide lots of options. When the learner fails to deal effectively with a situation, a relevant story about it can be displayed; the learner can choose to bypass the story and try again; he or she can do some data gathering; the learner can ask a coach for help. It's more work to program alternative paths through scenarios, but it's critical. Throughout the simulation, people should be able to make the same choices they'd make in a real situation. If they're forced to make artificial choices, all they're learning is how to play the game.

- **Keep it complex**. This may violate training's unofficial motto, "Keep it simple, stupid," but simple isn't real. There are plenty of simplistic simulations out there, the sort of tapes in which the customer says, "Yes, I'll buy" as soon as the sales trainee makes the obvious pitch. A lot of the simulations ask the trainee to choose between A and B, turning learning into an either-or exercise. This is reminiscent of the computer game called Pick-Up from years ago, the object of which was to try to pick up four computerized women with the right line. Each woman was programmed to respond to a certain approach. The redhead liked her men to be aggressive; the librarian-type preferred a more refined pitch. This game is exactly like the simple-minded simulations in today's marketplace. One reason it takes an LSC team a month to build an hour's simulation is because the designers are sticklers for details. For instance, they factor in the details of personality when they build scenarios. People in the scenario are programmed to react in a variety of ways, depending on how the trainees approach them. The "redheads" don't just say yes when the trainee approaches them aggressively; they have various possible responses to a variety of approaches. Real life contains numerous possibilities, and good simulation designers try to simulate as many of them as they can.

SCRIPTING INTERESTING FAILURES

Trainers can create a realistic simulation built on the stories of a number of experts and still produce ineffective training. The trainers may even build the simulations around failures and find the simulations don't impart the desired skills. What people forget is that there are all sorts of failures and all sorts of ways of experiencing it. Think about failing a subject at school. Maybe your classmate failed algebra because she found it excruciatingly dull. Or perhaps another student failed a science course because the tests were ridiculously difficult. In either case, the student didn't learn from the failure because the failure wasn't made interesting.

When people screw up during simulations they find to be dull, they don't store the facts or lessons from the failure in their memory. But it's not just dullness that can short-circuit learning. It may be that the designer tied the failure to something trainees believe to be trivial: The simulation failed to answer the telephone properly. Or it may be that the failure doesn't catalyze learning because the failure was deemed unfair. For instance, the learner messes up and feels like he or she was tricked into failing—like playing a rigged game. All this trainee ultimately learns is how to win the game (rather than acquire the underlying skill). Or it may be that the failure seems irrelevant. The learner doesn't care about the failure because it doesn't seem to have much bearing on the skill to be learned.

Creating Simulations in Which People Fail Naturally

All of these failures are uninteresting, at least from a learning perspective. What the mind finds interesting are failures that are unexpected, that catch participants by surprise. These are the failures that are remembered. For this reason, the trainer wants to give people every opportunity to make the mistakes they would invariably make on the job. The trainer sets up learners to make choices that seem right but turn out to be wrong. Recall that in the Systimax program for Anixter, the scenario caused many trainees to plow through the selling process without bringing in a representative from Anixter's partner, Lucent, as they were supposed to do. Only when the customer complained that a Lucent representative was not brought in did trainees realize the failure. It's an interesting one because it really does catch participants by surprise—they are so focused on the customer that they forget about this partner. Until that point, trainees thought everything was going along smoothly. The failure ambushed them, and they're not likely to forget it.

In using the computer simulation for bartender trainees, Bennigans people fail in an interesting way. As stated earlier, one purpose of the simulation is to provide bartenders with the knowledge and tools necessary to do a good job of selling Bennigans' 300 beers. Bennigans found that on the job, bartenders don't push this 300-beer promotion. During customer interactions, they avoid situations that have to do with this promotion; they're overwhelmed by the prospect of promoting 300 beers and therefore don't tell customers about it. Although the restaurant manager can point out this failure to bartenders on the job, they won't learn from it. No one likes to fail in public. If a restaurant manager happened to chew out a bartender for this misdeed, the bartender would probably respond by pinning his failure on the manager ("He's a jerk; he couldn't sell 300 beers either") rather than thinking about what he did wrong.

Interesting failures cause people to think about how and why they made a mistake. In the Bennigans' simulation, for instance, bartenders experience situations where they fail because they lack knowledge. It's not personal; they're not accused of being stupid; and it's private. When a bartender is on the job and someone asks about some esoteric Italian beer the bartender knows nothing about, the natural impulse is to avoid the situation. When it happens in a computer simulation, the trainee thinks, "Hmmm. Why don't I know anything about that Italian beer?" And this person is motivated to find out. People hate not to know facts about their jobs. It's human nature. When employees fail in private because they lack knowledge, it's an interesting failure that motivates them to seek the knowledge they lack.

Failure Ceases to Be Interesting If It Becomes Constant

Remember the concept of expectation failure: When trainees don't expect to fail, they learn from it. But if people fail repeatedly, they expect to fail. When that mentality starts, learning stops. In many organizations, people fail constantly at their jobs. Some of them get away with it because there aren't any significant consequences for failure. In other instances, many of these people expect and accept their constant failures and don't even think about them. In a computer simulation, trainers want people to fail but not to repeat their failures. If trainers set up scenarios that are absurdly difficult or that trick participants or that haven't provided good explanations for learners' failures and resources to draw on, the trainers are inviting constant and uninteresting failure.

GOOD PRODUCTION VALUES

This book has drawn a number of analogies between computer simulations and movies. That's because the techniques required to create both media are similar. The following production tips enhance the effectiveness of simulations:

- **Create dramatic and entertaining scenarios**. This is not an instructional video. It's not traditional training translated to software. For the simulation to work, it needs to have the same elements of any good movie: quality writing, acting, and production. The script should draw people into the scenario, involving them emotionally and intellectually. There should be dramatic moments; humor is great. Designers want believable actors to play key parts (such as the coach in the Andersen simulation). Above all else, the script never should *tell* trainees what managers want them to know. Bad simulations, like bad art, preach at the audience.

- **Be willing to edit**. Some scripts don't work as well on film as they do on paper. There are times when it's necessary to reshoot scenes and revise scripts. Don't assume that it's okay if a scene doesn't work well, that "this isn't Hollywood." It might not be Hollywood, but the program is still playing to an audience of amateur critics. It's worth the effort to get a simulation right, even if it causes some delays.

- **Consider the possibility of sequels**. Many organizations find that changing circumstances dictate a new version of an old simulation. For instance, LSC creates a simulation for Company A on selling one particular product, and two years later the company wants another simulation revolving around another product. If the first one was created with an eye toward sequels, it's probable that the organization can reuse the original simulation just by editing out some material and filming and editing in new stuff. Modularity is another way of describing this technique.

- **Get the stars to the set on time**. In this case, the stars are the experts. It's not that they're prima donnas. It's just that as experts, they're in great demand throughout the organization and are often on the road when trainers need them to be interviewed. These experts kick-start the process of putting scenarios together; they give learners insight about failures related to the skill the company wants its people to acquire. If the key experts aren't there at the beginning, the team won't make much progress no matter how many other people you interview.

TRAINERS DON'T NEED BRILLIANT (AND EXPENSIVE) PROGRAMMERS TO MAKE GREAT SIMULATIONS

Most companies can't afford the best programmers every time they need a computer simulation, or they can't acquire top programmers' services because they're too busy. That's why ILS labored so long to create tools that most companies can use to produce these simulations. Those tools—ASK, MOP-ED, and GuSS—are nothing more than models that guide people as they put together simulations. I'm not claiming that these are the definitive models or that at some point in the future trainers won't come out with new and improved models.

The ASK Tool

As the name suggests, the ASK tool helps companies construct systems that provide easy access to experts. The resulting systems usually contain multimedia databases (videos and text), enabling users to ask questions of experts in relevant fields. Some organizations use these systems to house "corporate memories" deemed important to cultures and money and provide direction.

ASK systems contain answers to the most likely questions to be asked by neophytes attempting to master a given skill. The trick in ASK systems is ease of navigation. Thousands of stories don't make the systems more difficult to use. In fact, a large number of stories enhance the experience in an ASK system.

MOP-ED

The MOP-ED tool helps designers build training scenarios in which the desired skill or behavior is well-known and easily defined. Organizations frequently use MOP-ED to help people acquire "hard" skills related to service positions—how to operate cash registers, answer customer complaints on the phone, and so on. MOP-ED is for procedural learning. If the procedure is well-defined, MOP-ED can be used to teach it.

GuSS

The Guided Social Simulation (GuSS) tool helps construct systems designed to teach complex social tasks—coaching, supervisory skills, and selling, among others. This is the most ambitious tool, in that it attempts to build a simulation around competencies that aren't always as well-defined or understood as the skills taught through MOP-ED. Typically, LSC teams use GuSS when the objective is for users to respond in different ways to different personalities.

These tools dovetail with the techniques described in this chapter and illustrated in the earlier case studies. When used together, the tools and techniques enable organizations to:

- Make skill-facilitating expertise always available to people.
- Teach simple and complex skills faster and more effectively than in any other type of training by placing people in virtual learning scenarios designed in accordance with how people really learn.

Best of all, these tools are only the beginning. In the colloquial words of an anonymous optimist, "You ain't seen nothin' yet."

12

CHAPTER

HOW TO START YOUR OWN TRAINING REVOLUTION

You've just experienced a training epiphany: You realize that much (if not all) of your training is worthless. It's a bit of a shock. If you take the words in this book as gospel, you're probably eager to build a virtual learning system. Even if you don't take these words as gospel—if you're intrigued but skeptical—you may want to test the virtual learning waters.

In either case, the question is: How?

The techniques of the previous chapter give you some guidelines for building a computer simulation, but if you're like most people, it's difficult to know where to begin. Some of the questions I frequently receive after giving a talk on this subject are:

- Should we create a computer simulation or a role-playing scenario?
- Should we put our company's MIS director in charge of building a simulation?
- Do we really have to get rid of all our old "telling" training; can't we salvage some of it?
- How likely is it that our organization has the expertise necessary to design virtual learning?
- Where are we most likely to get stuck and struggle if we attempt to do what you suggest?

Here are some answers to these and other questions that will help your company move in the right direction.

PHASE OUT EXISTING TRAINING MATERIALS

Examine your training for "passivities" (as opposed to activities). Look for:

- Classroom lectures
- Materials meant to be read and studied
- Computer-based "learning" that puts the lectures and reading materials on a screen
- Multiple-choice tests
- Distance learning (where the lecture comes via satellite)

Phase all this stuff out. Yes, that's a radical step because it may leave you with precious little training. On the other hand, what are you really losing if you convert your classrooms to computer labs and burn your manuals?

A month down the road, people won't remember much of what they're forced to memorize or what they're told. They'll remember even less if the telling is pedantic and boring.

This doesn't mean that the information you attempt to communicate in your training is worthless; it's the delivery system that needs fixing. Certainly some hard-won knowledge can be salvaged. If you have lecturers who tell great stories, you can salvage those stories and incorporate them into a simulation or a role-play. If you've compiled lots of information about how to do a given job effectively (and how people do it ineffectively), you can translate that into virtual learning activities. Instead of telling a salesperson that better results are achieved through cold calls made on the phone rather than through letter or fax, you can let her discover this important fact herself. Or perhaps you can set up a role-playing situation where she'll opt for sending a letter and fail; that's when your advice about using the phone will have impact.

It's also possible that some of your training can be taken out of the classroom and applied on-the-job. You may be missing opportunities to let people learn by looking over someone's shoulder. If the logistics are right, your experts may be able to help neophytes learn in an informal apprenticeship. Although apprenticeships are impractical for many companies, they may be an overlooked learning method for others. Apprenticeships seem hopelessly old-fashioned, and some companies have been too quick to discard them in favor of trendy business universities and multimedia learning.

By eliminating your current training methodology, you're not eliminating all the precious knowledge it attempts to convey. Throwing out the baby with the bathwater isn't necessary.

SOME ROLE-PLAYING ADVICE

Probably many people in your organization are capable of creating a goal-based, role-playing scenario. They may not, however, be capable of creating an effective scenario because they make the following three mistakes:

- Miss the main point.
- Cast the wrong people for the right roles.
- Focus on dialogues.

To help you produce effective role-plays, let's look at each of these "failures" and suggest the proper way to go about this process.

Design Virtual Learning to Stick to the Point

Missing the main point means that the role-play scenario tries to do too much; it's designed to impart 14 lessons to role-players rather than one key lesson. Identifying the skill you really want your people to acquire and designing the scenario around it will greatly enhance the scenario's effectiveness.

Get a Believable Person for Each Role

The second mistake—casting the wrong people for roles—is a crucial factor discussed earlier. I could tell people a hundred times not to cast a junior executive as a CEO or a trainer as a master salesperson and I'd still be ignored. People think anyone can "play" these parts, and the problem is that few people can play them realistically. You want the reactions of the people in these roles to be authentic, to duplicate the reactions you'd find in real-life situations.

By doing this, you learn how to handle an irate customer or to coach an underachieving subordinate. Rather than spending money on hiring outside trainers and printing big, fat manuals, spend it on hiring retired CEOs, downsized executives, and other experts to fill your roles.

Encourage Multiple Routes to Learning

The third mistake is a killer of good scenarios. When you sit down to create a scenario, your tendency may be to create dialogues—you lay out a situation designed to get the trainee to respond with words. For instance, your scenario involves a sales situation in which the customer says no, and you want to teach the trainee how to keep pushing after the first rejection.

So your scenario calls for the customer to say no and for the trainee to think of something to say to keep the sales call alive. There's not much work for the trainee to do but respond with the first thing that comes to mind.

Good scenarios are more elaborate than this. They encourage trainees to do some investigation before offering their verbal response to the situation. Well-constructed virtual learning gives learners the chance to ask questions of an expert; it gives them the option of looking up information on a computer or hearing someone tell a story. These "props" may be conspicuously displayed in the scenario to encourage their use; they're probably more visible than they would be in a real-life dilemma.

The objective is for people to push and probe on their own in order to solve a problem. It's fine to let learners flail about as they pursue a potential solution. All of this trial-and-error encourages self-explanation.

Probing on their own (rather than hearing the answers from others) to achieve a goal is important. If there's anything worthwhile about the educational model, it's the notion of homework (what's not worthwhile is that the homework is often memorization of trivial facts). People tend to remember papers they slaved over; papers that involved research, drawing conclusions, and formulating new ideas. Therefore, if you decide to create a role-playing scenario on your own, make sure it includes the equivalent of interesting homework assignments that cause people to dig, question, and self-explain.

SOME COMPUTER SIMULATION ADVICE

Again, let's approach this from the negative standpoint of mistakes commonly made. The two big mistakes are:

- Putting an MIS person or programmer in charge of the project
- Creating simulations that bear only a faint resemblance to real human behavior

Who's in Charge?

The first mistake should be expected. The organizational logic is: If it has to do with computers, put a computer person in charge. The problem, of course, is that most MIS people don't know much about learning.

As a result, programmers tend to create simulations that are technologically rich and learning-poor. It's obvious that a programmer is running the show when the simulation turns out to be a game. These computer games may offer the illusion of learning: they're fun to play and are cleverly constructed around work situations. They don't, however, teach anyone much of anything except how to win the computer game. Programmers take the dictum, "Learning should be fun," too much to heart. Remember: Just because it's fun doesn't mean it's learning.

At the same time, the solution isn't always to put a training person in charge. Some trainers merely want to turn their manuals and classrooms into software; they see computers as an opportunity to jazz up their telling approach with eye-catching graphics and other bells and whistles. You can spot this type of training program a mile off; it invariably starts with a long-winded introduction telling people exactly what they need to learn.

The right person to put in charge is someone who endorses the learning-by-doing concept. They come from different backgrounds—Ph.D.'s in education, artificial intelligence, or cognitive psychology—and they understand basic principles of learning. If you find someone in your company who despises the educational model and appreciates apprenticeships, you've probably found your person.

Using the Shades of Gray

The other mistake has to do with simulating real human behavior. Some organizations embark on computer simulations with the best of learning intentions but lack the skill necessary to do them effectively. This is especially true when they're trying to create social simulations. Human interactions are filled with ambiguities, paradoxes, and myriad possibilities.

The mistake that's made is to simplify these interactions to the point that there's nothing human about them—they are black-and-white issues. Trainees look at these simulations and immediately dismiss them as "just another stupid training exercise."

Instead, designers must recognize the need for some level of verisimilitude. Although many organizations lack the expertise to produce completely realistic simulations, most can build in enough reality that they're not laughable.

When trainers design simulations, it is wise to keep in mind that people react in different ways to the same situation. Taking this fact into account in building simulations, branches of the program can offer a variety of responses from which trainees can choose.

WHATEVER YOU DO, HAVE PEOPLE *DO* SOMETHING

Regardless of whether a company decides to create a role-playing scenario or a computer simulation, trainers will be tempted to start by listing the program's "learning objectives."

Resist that temptation! At least, don't compose a list consisting of pieces of knowledge that must be acquired by trainees. If one of the objectives is for trainees to acquire "a thorough understanding of Company ABC's procedures for dealing with customer complaints," the training will be constrained by that knowledge-acquisition objective. Even if the trainer wants to create goal-based scenarios, he or she won't be able to. The teaching mission will become making sure people have those procedures memorized. It will be the mission adopted because of measurement devices that test how well people remember those procedures.

If you must compose a learning objectives list, place only "doing verbs" on that list. In other words, all objectives relate to what people can do when they complete training, not the facts and numbers they remember. If the trainer must create a measurement device, have it measure what people can do via observation. If the objective is handling an irate customer, the assessor should observe whether a given trainee is able to handle irate customers in the store. Be careful not to cheat in writing objectives. For instance: "Trainees must know the 24 steps required so they can repair our engines." The word *know* cheats on the task trainees must do. People may know the 24 steps but be incapable of repairing engines. The right way to phrase the objective is: "Trainees must be able to repair our engines."

There are all sorts of ways to learn by doing. For instance, one company teaches its people to answer phones by monitoring how they answer "staged" calls. When novices fail to answer the phones effectively, the monitor intervenes. The point is that the role-playing scenarios and computer simulations discussed in this book aren't the only alternatives (and as the next chapter points out, there will probably be many new options in the future). Variations on the apprenticeship theme exist that can be used successfully. As trainers attempt to create virtual learning programs, they should keep their options open.

SOME GUIDING QUESTIONS

As you should understand by this point, this book is not going to give you 20 steps to build a virtual learning training program. Nor does it offer a model or diagram that helps you chart your course through the obstacles of building such a program. Locking you into such a rigid structure would be the same as standing over you and saying, "Do this first, then do this, then do this." If you're going to learn to build virtual learning into your training, you need to model the learning style by flailing about, going in the wrong direction, and asking yourself what went wrong.

Still, as you might recall from earlier chapters, nobody wants learners to become so frustrated and depressed by their failures that they give up. That's why good simulations include online help when trainees get stuck; that's when they choose to hear a story related to their failure or have a coach give them some ideas. In lieu of that, for your own groundwork in virtual learning, you can address the following series of questions as you develop new training:

- Are trainees motivated to learn what we want to teach them?
- Are the best, most instructive stories about our company being incorporated into the training?
- Are we making sure our training gives people the chance to fail in natural, unexpected ways?
- What percentage of time do trainees spend passively listening and reading?
- At what point do we tell trainees stories and give them other forms of coaching; is it just in time (right after they fail when they're primed to explain the failure) or is it random?

- Is the training experience enjoyable, entertaining, and challenging, or is it burdensome, boring, and routine?
- Are we trying to teach a skill that we have no experience with or expertise in (such as training people to run a new computer system)?
- Are we asking people to fail in front of others or in private?
- Are we enabling our people to discover things on their own and teach themselves?

13
CHAPTER

HOW PEOPLE WILL LEARN IN THE FUTURE

The learning revolution is still in its infancy. The organizations that are using computer simulations and role-playing scenarios as part of their training are today's pioneers. They are the first to recognize that traditional training methods don't work, who are not only embracing computer technology as a learning tool but the principles of expectation failure, goal-based scenarios, and the truly revolutionary notion that learning should be fun.

The future of organizational training no doubt will be determined by how effective these organizations become in training their people. Right now, there is compelling empirical evidence that the training is effective. Various formal and informal surveys have provided that evidence, and the time and cost savings are self-evident. Still, the pioneering individuals within these companies sometimes encounter resistance. You can't have a revolution without such obstacles as the old guard, the status quo, and cries of "These radical ideas are dangerous!" It's a mistake to underestimate resistance to new ideas or the impact this resistance might have on how quickly they're adopted.

Where the virtual learning revolution is headed is anyone's guess. This concluding chapter represents my best guess.

BUILD IT AND THEY WILL COME

After the Institute for the Learning Sciences helped Andersen construct its Business Practices Course (BPC) and Andersen had been using the simulation for a while, an interesting thing happened. Other companies started inquiring about purchasing the BPC simulation and using it to teach their own people business practices. These companies had no problem with the fact that it was created specifically for Andersen; they reasoned (correctly) that a basic business skill was a basic business skill. Andersen wasn't interested in selling its proprietary materials, but the point is that other companies were eager to buy them.

In the future, trainers will see a lot more of this. There are a finite number of skills that organizations want to teach—selling, managing, customer service, and so on. Right now, organizations have to create simulations from scratch to teach these skills. In the future, they will be able to buy "generic" or prepackaged software, saving a great deal of money and time in the process. Imagine a simulation on selling business-to-business office supplies in which the world's leading sales experts in this area contribute their stories; where the simulation is based on their expertise and experience. Over time, every type of simulation imaginable will be created. After that, it's logical to assume that companies won't attempt to reinvent the wheel—they'll simply pick and choose the best simulation from the 10 packages on the market.

"But wait," the A student in the front row might protest. "How can a generic goal-based scenario possibly capture our unique corporate culture, the special situations we face, the unusual market position?"

Trainers can capture these flavors by modifying the generic packages to meet the corporation's particular needs. Although companies *do* differ in certain respects, they are generally more similar than they think. Just about every organization wants to maintain a high degree of integrity and profitability; just about every company believes in adding value, in respecting others, in accountability. The differences that exist—one company believes in highly aggressive selling techniques, whereas another has an open and antiauthoritarian culture—can be accommodated by modifying simulations. In fact, companies won't just be buying software for people to load in computers; they'll be buying templates that can be adapted for a company's specific needs and concerns.

This view of the future brings up a logical question. If, at some point in the future, all these electronic tools eliminate classrooms and manuals, what happens to the training department?

THE CHANGING ROLE OF TRAINERS

Training people aren't dooming themselves by embracing virtual learning (in fact, they would doom themselves by rejecting it, because their competitors will embrace it and create superior training). Trainers will, however, find themselves taking on a different role within the organization. Trainers as the business counterpart to school teachers will soon be an outmoded concept. The ability to bring the training to people rather than bring the people to training will relieve training managers of the logistical and coordination responsibilities that currently take so much of their time.

Instead, the role of training managers will be to acquire the right courses, make sure the right people take the right courses, and modify those courses to fit the designs of the organization. This last responsibility will be critical. The ability to customize software will save organizations enormous amounts of money. Instead of buying one new piece of software after another, trainers will modify a generic program for reuse. Shaping software to fit changing business requirements, services, and products will be a highly prized skill, and the training people who master that skill will be extraordinarily valuable.

Not every training person out there will jump up and down with joy at this prospect. Some training managers with educational backgrounds avoid multimedia-based training, especially when goal-based scenarios (as opposed to lecturing and testing) are involved. On the other hand, the training people who have worked with institute teams recognize the bankruptcy of traditional methods and the advantages conferred by technology. To ignore the possibilities of computer simulations is akin to insisting that the typing pool continue to use old manual typewriters rather than word processing software.

BETTER-TRAINED, MORE MOTIVATED ENTRY-LEVEL PEOPLE

One of the less obvious but highly significant ramifications of the developments described throughout this book is better employees. Right now, many new college graduates have no idea what they want to do; many of them even get advanced degrees and are still in the dark about careers. Consciously or not, they end up sampling a number of careers, taking a job, quitting it after a year and trying a new one. The problem with this, as every organization can attest, is a largely uninspired entry-level employee. No matter how great the training is, it doesn't have much impact. The assumption of virtual learning is that an employee wants to learn to do a job better for personal satisfaction and career advancement. If an employee is bored and just putting in time until he or she finds a real career calling, the employee is not going to master the skills required or will do a mediocre job of learning them.

In the future, however, people will have access to the same generic skill software as organizations do. Individuals will buy (or more likely, check out of the library) five simulations of jobs in different industries. They can encounter the situations and practice the skills that would be required as a sporting-goods salesperson, a computer programmer, a lawyer, and an accountant. After trial-and-error use of such simulations, high-school-aged students will have a much better sense of the type of jobs they enjoy doing. Just as important, they'll have acquired some of the key skills for jobs in their chosen field. It might even be possible that they will have gone through the same simulation a prospective employer uses to train new hires. The organization's trainers may modify the standard simulations for this "pre-trained" entry-level worker to help him or her gain more sophisticated skills or let such a novice skip ahead to simulations for people with a few years of experience.

What will these simulations be like? Will they resemble the ones described in this book? Yes, in some ways. But just as computer software become more sophisticated with each new generation, so will simulations move to a higher level.

THE REAL THING

In predicting that the simulations will become more sophisticated, I don't mean simply more bells and whistles. Yes, the animation in Andersen's Zed simulation is neat and everyone always oohs and ahs over how the user can summon a talking coach to the computer screen to provide ideas and advice. But real sophistication in these simulations has to do with reality— how close the designer can come to the perfect simulation.

Think about a flight simulator. The best ones simulate reality to the *n*th degree. When the user steers right, the simulator angles itself to the right. When the user fails to avoid a storm, the simulator shakes just as it would amid real turbulence. Short of bursting into flames when the user flies into a mountain, the flight simulator captures the experience of flying with uncanny accuracy.

In the future, training simulations will do the same. The goal will be to make trainees feel like they have somehow entered into a virtual workplace where the encounters are completely believable. People will get into arguments with co-workers and forget (for a little while, at least) that the co-workers are computer-generated. At some point, the characters users interact with may be three-dimensional and live in a virtual reality so real that it is entirely compelling. But even if the technology doesn't enable training to advance to this stage, it will permit users to have much more realistic personal interactions.

Although today's simulations are good at approximating real interactions with bosses, consultants, suppliers, and others, the programs are still somewhat limited. Right now, designers can program a "character" in a simulation to respond in only a few ways, depending on what the trainee does. In real life, however, that character might respond in any one of 100 ways. Designers are going to be able to create simulations that offer all those possibilities. It will be possible to create characters that respond in so many identifiable ways that the trainee will interact with them just as they would with a real human.

That reality will increase the effectiveness of the training. The closer trainers get to duplicating the feelings and thoughts of a real expectation failure, the better the simulations will help people acquire targeted skills.

WHAT'S DRIVING THIS ELECTRONIC FUTURE

Some CEOs and other top executives aren't overly concerned about these issues. For them, training pales in importance next to financial issues, new markets, and breakthrough technologies. If you're a chief executive reading this, you're probably thinking, "Yes, I know, the HR guys have already told me: People are our most important asset."

Wrong. To twist the slogan from President Clinton's first election campaign: "It's not the people, stupid."

It's the *knowledge*.

What organizations know will provide them with their single most important competitive edge. Though there's a lot of truth in that statement today, it will be the rule of thumb in the future. Years ago, people bought goods from one shopkeeper's store and not a competitor's because the shopkeeper had merchandise the other one lacked. Perhaps the shopkeeper went to considerable effort to obtain this merchandise; maybe that shopkeeper even made it. My mother and grandfather ran a bead importing business in New York; they sold beads to people who used them as part of jewelry or pocketbook designs. My mother traveled to Europe and Japan and brought back the beads she thought her customers would want. Her competitive edge was her ability to buy the right beads.

Today, that's not much of an edge. Just about everyone has similar products. Consumers don't even have to go to the store to buy most products; purchasers order from television direct response commercials or catalogs using a toll-free number. Or the computer-literate consumer can do a complete transaction on the Internet. Brand loyalty is decreasing, most products adhere to the same quality standards, and price is dependent on optional features. At some point there won't be *any* significant differences between products or services in the same category (and some might say that advertising is responsible for many of the perceived differences today).

When companies are no longer able to sell on brand loyalty, quality, or price, what's left? In a world of parity products, where does one get an edge? From knowledge, of course. What organizations know about service, about selling, about supervising, and about process requirements is what counts. For instance, your sales experts may have discovered some invaluable truths about how to handle certain situations that always arise in selling specific types of products to specific types of customers. The experts gained this expertise through years of experience; experience that upstart competitors don't have or that old-line companies never developed. Having this knowledge gives one company the potential for an edge; disseminating the knowledge quickly, effectively, and cost-efficiently cinches it.

Everything else is details. A company may come up with great product promotions, terrific five-year strategies, and eye-catching packaging. But if managers don't give their people the knowledge and skills they need to sell and service customers, the other stuff won't matter. (And it can be argued that a company's employees aren't going to come up with great promotions, strategies, and packaging unless managers help them acquire the skills to do so.)

Training will become more important for another reason. Though products may achieve parity status, there will be more of them and more sophisticated ones than ever before. The investment in R&D and all the new technologies will produce a wide range of complex products, especially in certain industries.

For instance, LSC is doing work for a pharmaceutical company that has an array of new medications. The team is constructing an ASK system for the company's salespeople that contains video clips of doctors talking about the drugs and how to use them effectively, stories from patients who have taken the drugs, and so on. The program for Bennigans' bartenders is built around stories and questions relating to their 300 beers. The information revolution is producing more data than people can hold. Organizing all this data and making it easily accessible is what ASK systems are all about: obtaining the exact information needed exactly when it's needed.

Employees can use these systems and simulations to keep vast quantities of often-complex information under control. It lets managers channel the flow of product knowledge where they want it to go. In an increasingly complex world, this ability is essential for every organization.

WHO WILL LEAD THE REVOLUTION?

To pose the question another way: What types of organizations will make the investment in developing these new systems? It's fine to gaze in a crystal ball and see a learning paradise, but this vision isn't worth much if it also doesn't encompass companies capable of taking the risks necessary to make things happen.

The Logistics

Don't minimize the risk. It's not going to be easy for an HR executive to go to management and say, "We want to invest x number of dollars in buying and modifying these computer simulations that are based on expectation failure and just-in-time storytelling, and we want them to replace all our classroom training and manuals." Right now it's tough enough to convince a company just to test a simulation for training people in one area. What indicates that the future is going to unfold as I suggest, however, is that large organizations will need a better, faster, and cheaper way to train their people. Not want, but need. Even now, leaders of big companies that are growing by leaps and bounds are frustrated by their training inadequacies. Clients talk about how they're opening new offices, stores, and plants all over the world. They have their expansion strategies down cold; they're highly proficient at building new factories; devising strategies to enter new markets; and operating restaurants, shoe stores, and discount chains. The skill they lack is equipping thousands of new hires with the knowledge and skills necessary to work effectively.

The logistical nightmare of disseminating expertise is daunting. Do companies bring everyone to a central training location and train them there, incurring huge costs in travel and lodging as well as taking up a great deal of experts' valuable time? Or do companies let novices loose on the job and hope they learn on their own with some rudimentary training as their only job preparation?

Neither alternative is attractive. And it's going to be even less attractive in the future as organizations increase the pace and scope of their global expansion. A basic truth will drive them toward computer simulations.

Companies That Get New People Productive Faster Will Become More Profitable

The ability to train people at their home office locations via a three-hour computer simulation is enormously appealing for many reasons, not the least of which is turnover. Nothing frustrates organization leaders more than spending a lot of money flying people all over the place, getting them trained only to see them leave a short time later, and then repeating this process.

The promise of computer simulations is twofold. First, although turnover rates may be high, simulations mean that training costs are relatively low—the computer simulation costs less the more it is used. Second, simulations may actually help reduce turnover. Though this is a debatable point, keep in mind that people like their jobs better when they know how to do them. Poorly trained people feel incompetent, and no one likes to feel that way. Well-trained people can do their jobs well, which is rewarding.

Although large companies probably will lead the virtual learning revolution, support will come from a variety of other places. For instance, right now small businesses don't do much multimedia-based training; they can't afford to. Small companies can't afford the investment required to build a simulation. In the future, however, they *will* be able to afford the generic simulation software that will be widely available. An entrepreneur opening a boutique that employees three people will be able to purchase software at minimal cost (maybe $500 to $1000) and help those three employees obtain the customer service skills they require.

The revolution won't be confined to the business world. Law firms, hospitals, and other service-based institutions will invariably jump on the bandwagon. In fact, LSC currently is building an ASK system to be used by doctors at a number of hospitals throughout the country. There are bound to be surgical simulations. This makes eminent sense in the same way that a flight simulator makes sense—people would rather that their pilot and their doctor make mistakes where they aren't fatal. Training lawyers through simulations is also a good idea; designers could simulate trial scenarios, deposition-taking, and client interactions. These are, of course, fairly sophisticated processes, and today designers are not at the technological level to produce simulations in these areas cost-effectively. There are so many variables involved in a lawyer-client interaction, for instance, that it would be difficult to capture the majority of them in a few hours of training. Programmers need more sophisticated tools to create such a scenario, and they're likely to have them in the next decade.

Universities will play a significant role in the development of these tools. Business schools are in an excellent position to create some of the generic business skill simulations. The business departments possess the knowledge (assuming they employ professors who are experts in key business competencies). Universities also should be motivated; they can use these simulations to educate their students and also sell them to companies (most new employees didn't go to their business school).

One caveat about all this: Ten years from now, employees will still learn the old-fashioned way, by apprenticeship. Some jobs will always be taught best by looking over an expert's shoulder. Some skills will be so esoteric that it won't make sense to construct virtual learning around them. On-the-job learning isn't going to disappear in the next century. It will, however, co-exist with virtual learning.

WHY THE ODDS AREN'T ON THE STATUS QUO

As for all predictions, certain pieces of the puzzle have to fall in place before they come true. Money is the big piece. Organizations are going to have to make an investment to build these simulations and purchase the hardware necessary to run them.

But money is also a catalyst for organizations to make that investment. When I talk about what I do, be it in speeches or to prospective clients, I focus on learning theory and the way the mind works. I talk about expectation failure, the way we label, store, and retrieve information, how learning should be fun, the use of stories, and so on. I explain how business training is modeled on our educational system, which doesn't work. I assume that organizations will recognize that they need to adapt learning theory to make their training more effective.

Perhaps corporate leaders buy that argument, but it's not what causes them to buy consulting services. Every organization is looking for ways to save money on training. The costs of flying everyone to a central training location and taking experts out of the field for training purposes drives managers nuts. It's not that they don't care about training effectiveness; it's that the costs are a much more tangible issue. When managers grasp the return on investment of computer simulations—how the portability of a disk can save a large company millions of dollars annually in training expenses—their eyes grow large.

As a business person, I'm pleased. As an academic, it's a bit disconcerting. I know that application of the ideas I have put forward here will greatly enhance training effectiveness. The amount of money more effective training will make for a company is incalculable (which I suppose is the problem). But what everyone wants to talk about is: "If we don't have to put 10,000 employees up in hotel rooms for a week each year or fly them out here, and if each of the senior people can produce an additional week of income because they don't have to teach, then. . . ."

The need to economize is understandable. It's what will make the future of virtual learning possible. Still, I also know what happens when companies like Andersen, Anixter, and Target put learning theory into practice: It works; the leaders become excited about the possibilities; they want to do more of it. People like John Smith at Andersen understand that computer simulations are more than tools to speed up the learning process and save money. They're all about effectiveness. Having more highly skilled employees than competitors have is what the future is all about. It's a virtual learning future that's approaching quickly, and the companies that have developed training programs around computer simulations and goal-based scenarios will be the ones that secure their place in that future.

I n d e x

A

abstraction of thought, 132
accommodate-customers skills, 120
actor selection for role-playing, 87,
150-151, 155-156
airlines, 2
Ameritech, 22
Andersen Consulting, xi-xii, 8, 9, 23,
47, 51, 53-65, 67-82, 121, 127, 128,
164
  Architecting Business Change
    simulation, 61-62
  Business Practices School (BPS),
    56, 81, 164
  business-skills training, 56-58
  coaching students, 59-61, 77
  complex skills training, 58-59,
    67-68
  cost of training, 54-55, 82
  customer service training, 72-76,
    74, 75, 76
  development time for simulations,
    82
  existing traditional training
    program, 53-55
  failures and mistakes, learning
    from, 61-63, 72-76, 76-79, 80-82
  frustration level vs. learning, 80-81
  Guided Social Simulation (GuSS)
    tool, 60, 152
  individualizing the simulation, 81
  information engineering training,
    58-59
  just-in-time training programs, 61
  learning by doing, 58-59, 72-79,
    80-81
  live simulations, 61-63
  management skills, 56-58

  measuring results, 64-65
  motivating students, 59-61, 68, 72
  multimedia systems, 54-55
  "reminding strategies" created by
    failures, 74
  requirements analysis training,
    70-71
  simulation design, 53, 61, 67-82,
    84-85
  skills vs. knowledge, 55-56, **56**
  story-gathering, 64, 76
  Tiger Electronics Scenario, 62-63
  video game concept as learning
    tool, 71-72, 80
  Zed's virtual restaurant
    simulation, 68-72, **69, 70**, 80, 127
Andersen, Arthur, xi
Anixter Inc. (*see also* sales training),
37, 51, 95-107
  choosing a computer-training
    system, 97-98
  coaching students, 102, 103-104
  complex skills training, 95
  corporate culture skills training,
    101-102
  "corporate memory" concept, 102,
    106-107
  cost of training, 95, 105
  designing simulations, 96-99
  experts behind the simulations, 106
  failures, learning from, 100-102,
    107
  flexibility/modularity of design,
    102
  Foundation Learning
    Architecture, 102
  implementing virtual learning
    system, 104-106
  learning by doing, 100-102

Illustrations are indicated in **boldface.**